C
INDIANA
BIRDS

Contributors:

Kenneth J. Brock, Krista Kagume, Gregory Kennedy

Lone Pine Publishing International

© 2007 Lone Pine Publishing International Inc.
First printed in 2007   10 9 8 7 6 5 4 3 2 1
Printed in China

Distributed by Lone Pine Publishing
1808 B Street NW, Suite 140
Auburn, WA USA 98001

Website: www.lonepinepublishing.com

Library and Archives Canada Cataloguing in Publication

Brock, Kenneth J.
   Compact guide to Indiana birds / Kenneth J. Brock, Krista Kagume, Gregory Kennedy.

Includes bibliographical references and index.
ISBN-13: 978-976-8200-27-3
ISBN-10: 976-8200-27-8

   1. Birds—Indiana—Identification. 2. Bird watching—Indiana.
I. Kennedy, Gregory, 1956– II. Kagume, Krista III. Title.

QL684.I5B76 2007   598.09772   C2006-905111-9

Illustrations: Gary Ross, Ted Nordhagen, Ewa Pluciennik
Cover Illustration: Northern Cardinal by Ted Nordhagen
Egg Photography: Alan Bibby, Gary Whyte
Scanning & Digital Film: Elite Lithographers Co.

PC: P13

Contents

Reference Guide.................... 4   *Introduction*...................... 10

Geese, Swans, Ducks 20

Turkeys, Quails.. 38

Grebes, Cormorants 42

Herons, Egrets, Vultures 46

Ospreys, Eagles, Harriers, Hawks, Kestrels, Falcons.. 54

Rails, Coots, Cranes 68

Plovers, Sandpipers, Woodcocks 74

Gulls, Terns.. 84

Pigeons, Doves, Cuckoos.. 96

Owls 104

Nightjars, Hummingbirds, Kingfishers.................... 110

Woodpeckers, Flickers.. 118

Wood-Pewees, Phoebes, Flycatchers, Kingbirds 128

Vireos 136

Jays, Crows.. 138

Larks, Swallows 142

Chickadees, Titmice, Nuthatches, Creepers, Wrens 150

Kinglets, Gnatcatchers, Bluebirds, Thrushes 162

Catbirds, Thrashers, Starlings, Waxwings.............. 172

Wood-warblers, Redstarts, Tanagers 182

Sparrows, Juncos, Cardinals, Buntings................... 196

Blackbirds, Meadowlarks, Cowbirds, Orioles 212

Finches, Old World Sparrows 222

Glossary.............................. 230   *Checklist*.......................... 232

Select References 237   *Index* 238

4 Reference Guide

Snow Goose
size 32 in • p. 20

Canada Goose
size 42 in • p. 22

Mute Swan
size 60 in • p. 24

Wood Duck
size 18 in • p. 26

Mallard
size 24 in • p. 28

Blue-winged Teal
size 15 in • p. 30

Lesser Scaup
size 17 in • p. 32

Common Goldeneye
size 18 in • p. 34

Hooded Merganser
size 17 in • p. 36

Wild Turkey
size 39 in • p. 38

Northern Bobwhite
size 10 in • p. 40

Pied-billed Grebe
size 14 in • p. 42

Double-crested Cormorant
size 29 in • p. 44

Great Blue Heron
size 53 in • p. 46

Great Egret
size 39 in • p. 48

Green Heron
size 18 in • p. 50

Turkey Vulture
size 28 in • p. 52

Osprey
size 23 in • p. 54

Bald Eagle
size 37 in • p. 56

Northern Harrier
size 20 in • p. 58

Cooper's Hawk
size 17 in • p. 60

Red-tailed Hawk
size 22 in • p. 62

American Kestrel
size 8 in • p. 64

Peregrine Falcon
size 18 in • p. 66

Sora
size 9 in • p. 68

American Coot
size 15 in • p. 70

Sandhill Crane
size 45 in • p. 72

Killdeer
size 10 in • p. 74

Lesser Yellowlegs
size 11 in • p. 76

Sanderling
size 8 in • p. 78

Pectoral Sandpiper
size 9 in • p. 80

American Woodcock
size 11 in • p. 82

Bonaparte's Gull
size 13 in • p. 84

Ring-billed Gull
size 19 in • p. 86

Herring Gull
size 25 in • p. 88

Caspian Tern
size 21 in • p. 90

BIRDS OF PREY

RAILS, COOTS & CRANES

SHOREBIRDS

GULLS & TERNS

GULLS & TERNS

Common Tern
size 15 in • p. 92

Forster's Tern
size 15 in • p. 94

Rock Pigeon
size 13 in • p. 96

DOVES & CUCKOOS

Eurasian Collared-Dove
size 13 in • p. 98

Mourning Dove
size 12 in • p. 100

Yellow-billed Cuckoo
size 12 in • p. 102

OWLS

Eastern Screech-Owl
size 9 in • p. 104

Great Horned Owl
size 23 in • p. 106

Barred Owl
size 21 in • p. 108

NIGHTJARS & HUMMINGBIRDS

Common Nighthawk
size 9 in • p. 110

Whip-poor-will
size 9 in • p. 112

Ruby-throated Hummingbird
size 4 in • p. 114

Belted Kingfisher
size 13 in • p. 116

Red-headed Woodpecker
size 9 in • p. 118

Red-bellied Woodpecker
size 10 in • p. 120

WOODPECKERS

Downy Woodpecker
size 7 in • p. 122

Northern Flicker
size 13 in • p. 124

Pileated Woodpecker
size 17 in • p. 126

Eastern Wood-Pewee
size 6 in • p. 128

Eastern Phoebe
size 7 in • p. 130

Great Crested Flycatcher
size 9 in • p. 132

Eastern Kingbird
size 9 in • p. 134

Red-eyed Vireo
size 6 in • p. 136

Blue Jay
size 12 in • p. 138

American Crow
size 19 in • p. 140

Horned Lark
size 7 in • p. 142

Purple Martin
size 8 in • p. 144

Tree Swallow
size 5 in • p. 146

Barn Swallow
size 7 in • p. 148

Carolina Chickadee
size 4 in • p. 150

Tufted Titmouse
size 6 in • p. 152

White-breasted Nuthatch
size 6 in • p. 154

Brown Creeper
size 5 in • p. 156

Carolina Wren
size 5 in • p. 158

House Wren
size 5 in • p. 160

Ruby-crowned Kinglet
size 4 in • p. 162

FLYCATCHERS

VIREOS

JAYS & CROWS

LARKS & SWALLOWS

CHICKADEES, NUTHATCHES & WRENS

KINGLETS, GNATCATCHERS & THRUSHES

8 Reference Guide

Blue-gray Gnatcatcher
size 4 in • p. 164

Eastern Bluebird
size 7 in • p. 166

Wood Thrush
size 8 in • p. 168

American Robin
size 10 in • p. 170

Gray Catbird
size 9 in • p. 172

Northern Mockingbird
size 10 in • p. 174

Brown Thrasher
size 11 in • p. 176

European Starling
size 8 in • p. 178

Cedar Waxwing
size 7 in • p. 180

Yellow Warbler
size 5 in • p. 182

Yellow-rumped Warbler
size 5 in • p. 184

Blackburnian Warbler
size 5 in • p. 186

American Redstart
size 5 in • p. 188

Ovenbird
size 6 in • p. 190

Common Yellowthroat
size 5 in • p. 192

Scarlet Tanager
size 7 in • p. 194

Eastern Towhee
size 8 in • p. 196

American Tree Sparrow
size 6 in • p. 198

Song Sparrow
size 7 in • p. 200

White-throated Sparrow
size 7 in • p. 202

White-crowned Sparrow
size 7 in • p. 204

Dark-eyed Junco
size 7 in • p. 206

Northern Cardinal
size 9 in • p. 208

Indigo Bunting
size 5 in • p. 210

Red-winged Blackbird
size 8 in • p. 212

Eastern Meadowlark
size 9 in • p. 214

Common Grackle
size 12 in • p. 216

Brown-headed Cowbird
size 7 in • p. 218

Baltimore Oriole
size 8 in • p. 220

Purple Finch
size 6 in • p. 222

House Finch
size 6 in • p. 224

American Goldfinch
size 5 in • p. 226

House Sparrow
size 6 in • p. 228

Introduction

If you have ever admired a songbird's pleasant notes, been fascinated by a soaring hawk or wondered about the identity of a songbird at your feeder, this book is for you. There is so much to discover about birds and their surroundings that birding is becoming one of the fastest growing hobbies on the planet. Many people find it relaxing, while others enjoy its outdoor appeal. Some people see it as a way to reconnect with nature, an opportunity to socialize with like-minded people or a way to monitor the environment.

Whether you are just beginning to take an interest in birds or can already identify many species, there is always more to learn. We've highlighted both the remarkable traits and the more typical behaviors displayed by some of our most abundant or noteworthy birds. A few birds live in specialized habitats, but most are common species that you have a good chance of encountering on most outings or in your backyard.

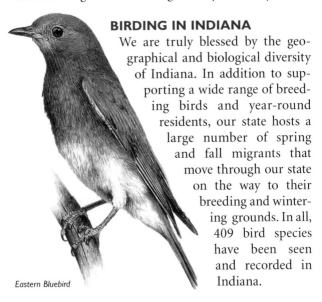

BIRDING IN INDIANA

We are truly blessed by the geographical and biological diversity of Indiana. In addition to supporting a wide range of breeding birds and year-round residents, our state hosts a large number of spring and fall migrants that move through our state on the way to their breeding and wintering grounds. In all, 409 bird species have been seen and recorded in Indiana.

Eastern Bluebird

Identifying birds in action and under varying conditions involves skill, timing and luck. The more you know about a bird—its range, preferred habitat, food preferences and hours and seasons of activity—the better your chances will be of seeing it. Generally, spring and fall are the busiest birding times. Temperatures are moderate then, many species of birds are on the move, and, in spring, male songbirds are belting out their unique courtship songs. Birds are usually most active in the early morning hours, except in winter when they forage while temperatures are at their mildest during the day.

Another useful clue for correctly recognizing birds is knowledge of their habitat. Simply put, a bird's habitat is the place where it normally lives. Some birds prefer open water, some are found in cattail marshes, others like mature coniferous forest, and still other birds prefer abandoned agricultural fields overgrown with tall grass and shrubs. Habitats are just like neighborhoods: if you associate friends with the suburb in which they live, you can easily learn to associate specific birds with their preferred habitat. Only in migration, especially during inclement weather, do some birds leave their usual habitat.

Recognizing birds by their songs and calls can greatly enhance your birding experience. Numerous tapes and CDs are available to help you learn bird songs, and a portable player with headphones can let you quickly compare a live bird with a recording. The old-fashioned way to remember bird songs is to make up words for them. We have given you some of the classic renderings in the species accounts that follow. Some of these approximations work better than others; birds often add or delete syllables from their calls, and very few pronounce consonants in a recognizable fashion. Remember, too, that songs may vary from place to place.

Indiana has a long tradition of friendly, recreational birding. In general, birders are willing to help beginners, share their knowledge and involve novices in their projects. Christmas bird counts, breeding bird surveys, nest box programs, migration monitoring, and birding lectures and workshops provide a chance for birders of all levels to interact and share the splendor of birds. Bird hotlines provide up-to-date information on the sightings of rarities, which are often easier to relocate than you might think. For more information or to participate in these projects, contact the following organizations:

Amos W. Butler Audubon Society
P.O. Box 80024
Indianapolis, IN 46280
Website: www.amosbutleraudubon.org
InfoLine/VoiceMail: (317) 767-4690

Indiana Audubon Society
Website: www.indianaaudubon.org
E-mail: indianaaudubon@yahoo.com

Dunes-Calumet Audubon Society
PO Box 447
Hammond, IN 46325-0447
Phone: (219) 931-4352

Sycamore Audubon Society
West Lafayette, IN
Website: www.sycamoreaudubon.org

BIRD LISTING
Many birders list the species they have seen during excursions or at home. It is up to you to decide what kind of list—systematic or casual—you will keep, and you may choose not to make lists at all. Lists may prove rewarding in unexpected ways, and after you visit a new

area, your list becomes a souvenir of your experiences there. Keeping regular, accurate lists of birds in your neighborhood can also be useful for local researchers. It can be interesting to compare the arrival dates and last sightings of hummingbirds and other seasonal visitors, or to note the first sighting of a new visitor to your area.

BIRD FEEDING

Many people set up bird feeders in their backyard, especially in winter. It is possible to attract specific birds by choosing the right kind of food and style of feeder. Keep your feeder stocked through late spring, because birds have a hard time finding food before flowers bloom, seeds develop and insects hatch. Contrary to popular opinion, birds do not become dependent on feeders, nor do they subsequently forget to forage naturally. Be sure to clean your feeder and the surrounding area regularly to prevent the spread of disease.

Landscaping your property with native plants is another way of providing natural food for birds. Flocks of waxwings have a keen eye for red mountain ash berries and hummingbirds enjoy columbine flowers. The cumulative effects of "nature-scaping" urban yards can be a significant step toward habitat conservation (especially when you consider that habitat is often lost in small amounts—a seismic line is cut in one area and a highway is built in another). Many good books and websites about attracting wildlife to your backyard are available.

NEST BOXES

Another popular way to attract birds is to put up nest boxes, especially for House Wrens, Eastern Bluebirds, Tree Swallows and Purple Martins. Not all birds will use nest boxes: only species that normally use cavities in trees are comfortable in such confined spaces. Larger nest boxes can attract kestrels, owls and cavity-nesting ducks.

CLEANING NEST BOXES AND FEEDERS

Nest boxes and feeding stations must be kept clean to prevent birds from becoming ill or spreading disease. Old nesting material may harbor a number of parasites. Once the birds have left for the season, remove the old nesting material and wash and scrub the nest box with detergent or a 10 percent bleach solution (1 part bleach to 9 parts water). You can also scald the nest box with boiling water. Rinse it well and let it dry thoroughly before you remount it.

Unclean bird feeders can become contaminated with salmonellosis and possibly other diseases. Seed feeders should be cleaned monthly; hummingbird feeders at least weekly. Any seed, fruit or suet that is moldy or spoiled must be discarded. Clean and disinfect feeding stations with a 10 percent bleach solution, scrubbing thoroughly. Rinse the feeder well and allow it to dry completely before refilling it. Discarded seed and feces on the ground under the feeding station should also be removed.

We advise that you wear rubber gloves and a mask when cleaning nest boxes or feeders.

WEST NILE VIRUS

Since the West Nile Virus first surfaced in North America in 1999, it has caused fear and misunderstanding. Some people have become afraid of contracting the disease from birds, and some health departments have advised residents to eliminate feeding stations and birdbaths.

To date, the disease has reportedly killed over 280 species of birds. Corvids (crows, jays and ravens) and birds of prey have been the most obvious victims because of their size, though the disease also affects some smaller species. The virus is transmitted among birds and to humans (as well as some other mammals) by mosquitoes that have bitten infected birds. Birds do not get the disease directly from other birds, and humans cannot get it from casual contact with infected birds. As well, not all mosquito species can carry the disease. According to the Centers for Disease Control and Prevention (CDC), only about 20 percent of people who are bitten and become infected will develop any symptoms at all and less than 1 percent will become severely ill.

Because mosquitoes breed in standing water, birdbaths have the potential to become mosquito breeding grounds. Birdbaths should be emptied and have the water changed at least weekly. Drippers, circulating pumps, fountains or waterfalls that keep water moving will prevent mosquitoes from laying their eggs in the water. There are also bird-friendly products available to treat water in birdbaths. Contact your local nature store or garden center for more information on these products.

ABOUT THE SPECIES ACCOUNTS

This book gives detailed accounts of 105 species of birds that can be expected in Indiana on an annual basis. The order of the birds and their common and scientific names follow the American Ornithologists' Union's Check-list of North American Birds (7th edition, July 1998, and its supplements through 2006).

As well as showing the identifying features of a bird, each species account also attempts to bring the bird to life by describing its various character traits. One of the challenges of birding is that many species look different in spring and summer than they do in fall and winter. Many birds have breeding and nonbreeding plumages, and immature birds often look different from their parents. This book does not try to describe or illustrate all the different plumages of a species; instead, it tries to focus on the forms that are most likely to be seen in our area.

ID: Large illustrations point out prominent field marks that will help you tell each bird apart. The descriptions favor easily understood language instead of technical terms.

Other ID: This section lists additional identifying features. Some of the most common anatomical features of birds are pointed out in the Glossary illustration (p. 231).

Size: The average length of the bird's body from bill to tail, as well as wingspan, are given and are approximate measurements of the bird as it is seen in nature. The size is sometimes given as a range, because there is variation between individuals, or between males and females.

Voice: You will hear many birds, particularly songbirds, which may remain hidden from view. Memorable paraphrases of distinctive sounds will aid you in identifying a species by ear.

Status: A general comment, such as "common," "uncommon" or "rare," is usually sufficient to describe the relative abundance of a species. Situations are bound to vary somewhat since migratory pulses, seasonal changes and centers of activity tend to concentrate or disperse birds.

Habitat: The habitats listed describe where each species is most commonly found. Because of the freedom that flight gives them, birds can turn up in almost any type of habitat. However, they will usually be found in environments that provide the specific food, water, cover and, in some cases, nesting habitat that they need to survive.

Similar Birds: Easily confused species are illustrated for each account. If you concentrate on the most relevant field marks, the subtle differences between species can be reduced to easily identifiable traits. But remember, even experienced birders can mistake one species for another.

Nesting: In each species account, nest location and structure, clutch size, incubation period and parental duties are discussed. A photo of the bird's egg is also provided. Remember that birding ethics discourage the disturbance of active bird nests. If you disturb a nest, you may drive off the parents during a critical period or expose defenseless young to predators.

Range Maps: The range map for each species shows the overall range of the species in an average year. Most birds will confine their annual movements to this range, although each year some birds wander beyond their traditional boundaries. The maps show breeding, summer and winter ranges, as well as migratory pathways—areas of the region where birds may appear while en route to nesting or winter habitat. The representations of the pathways do not distinguish high-use migration corridors from areas that are seldom used.

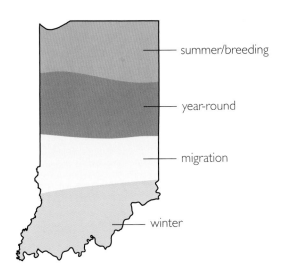

summer/breeding

year-round

migration

winter

TOP BIRDING SITES

From Lake Michigan to the Ohio River, Indiana can be divided into three natural regions: the Northern Region, the Central Till Plain and the Southern Unglaciated Area. Each region is composed of a number of different habitats that support a wealth of wildlife.

There are hundreds of good birding areas throughout our region. The following areas have been selected to represent a broad range of bird communities and habitats, with an emphasis on accessibility.

Northern Indiana
Sites on the Lakefront
1. Michigan City Harbor
2. Beverly Shores
3. Indiana Dunes SP
4. West Beach (Indiana Dunes NL)
5. Miller Beach
6. Hammond Lakefront Sanctuary
7. Forsythe Park
8. Whiting Park

Inland Sites
9. Fox Island Park, Fort Wayne
10. Salamonie Reservoir & State Forest
11. Kankakee FWA
12. Grand Kankakee Marsh (southern Lake County)
13. Kankakee Sands Preserve
14. Willow Slough FWA
15. Jasper-Pulaski FWA
16. Pine Creek Gamebird Habit Area

Central Indiana
17. Summit Lake SP
18. Mulvey Pond, Tippecanoe County
19. Eagle Creek Park
20. Fort Harrison SP
21. Universal Mine
22. Shades SP & Pine Hill Reserve
23. Turkey Run SP
24. Brookville Reservoir

Southern Indiana
25. Lake Monroe area
26. Lake Lemon
27. Muscatatuck NWR
28. Lake Gibson & Cane Ridge
29. Hawthorne Mine
30. Beehunter Marsh, Greene County
31. Ayrshire Mine & Bluegrass FWA
32. Lincoln SP

FWA = Fish and Wildlife Area
NL = National Lakeshore

NWR = National Wildlife Range
SP = State Park

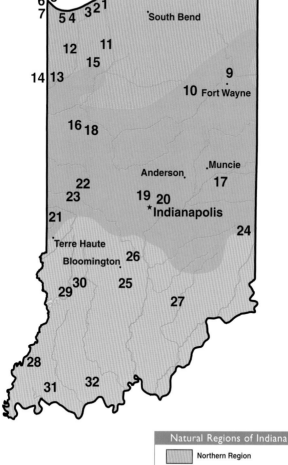

6 8
7 5 4 3 2 1
South Bend

12 11
15

14 13

9
10 Fort Wayne

16 18

Anderson. .Muncie
17

22
23 19 20
★Indianapolis

21

24

.Terre Haute
Bloomington 26
29 30 25
27

28
31 32

Natural Regions of Indiana

Northern Region

Central Till Plain

Southern Unglaciated Area

Snow Goose
Chen caerulescens

Noisy flocks of Snow Geese can be quite entertaining, creating a moving patchwork in the sky with their black wing tips and white plumage. • These geese breed in the Arctic, some traveling as far as northeastern Siberia and crossing the Bering Strait twice a year. Their smiling, serrated bills are made for grazing on short arctic tundra and for gripping the slippery roots of marsh plants. • Snow Geese can fly at speeds of up to 20 miles per hour. They are also strong walkers, and mothers have been known to lead their goslings up to 45 miles on foot in search of suitable habitat.

Other ID: head often stained rusty red.
Blue morph: white head and upper neck; dark blue-gray body.
Size: L 30–33 in; W 4½–5 ft.
Voice: loud, nasal, *houk-houk* in flight, higher pitched and more constant than the Canada Goose's call.
Status: abundant in southwestern Indiana in February and March.
Habitat: croplands, fields, estuarine marshes.

Similar Birds

Ross's Goose   Tundra Swan   Mute Swan
(p. 24)

Blue morph

black wing tips

dark "grin"
on bill

Nesting: does not nest in Indiana; nests in the
Arctic; female builds a nest lined with grass,
feathers and down; creamy white eggs are
3⅛ x 2 in; female incubates 4–7 eggs for
22–25 days.

Did You Know?

Some fall migrants fly
nonstop from James Bay,
Ontario, to the Texas
Gulf Coast.

Look For

Snow Geese fly in wavy,
disorganized lines, whereas
Canada Geese fly in a
V-formation. Occasionally
mixed flocks form in
migration.

Canada Goose

Branta canadensis

Canada Geese mate for life and are devoted parents. Unlike most birds, geese stay together in a family group for nearly a year, which increases the survival rate of the young. • Rescuers who care for injured geese report that these birds readily adopt their human caregivers. However, wild geese can be aggressive, especially when defending their young or competing for food. Hissing sounds and low, outstretched necks are signs that you should give these birds some space. • The Canada Goose was split into two species in 2004. The larger subspecies are still known as Canada Geese, while some smaller subspecies have been renamed Cackling Geese.

Other ID: dark brown upperparts; light brown underparts. *In flight:* flocks fly in V-formation.
Size: *L* 3–4 ft; *W* up to 6 ft.
Voice: loud, familiar *ah-honk*.
Status: abundant.
Habitat: lakeshores, riverbanks, ponds, farmlands and city parks.

Similar Birds

Cackling Goose

Greater White-fronted Goose

white "chin strap"

long, black neck

short, black tail

white undertail coverts

Nesting: usually on the ground; female builds a nest of grass and mud, lined with down; white eggs are 3½ x 2¼ in; female incubates 3–8 eggs for 25–28 days.

Did You Know?

Geese graze on aquatic grasses and sprouts, and you can spot them in the water, tipping up to grab for aquatic roots and tubers.

Look For

Large flocks of Canada Geese return to Indiana in February, and the first downy goslings of the year normally appear in late April.

Mute Swan
Cygnus olor

Admired for its grace and beauty, this Eurasian native was introduced to eastern North America in the mid-1800s to adorn estates, zoos and city parks. Several escaped from captivity in New Jersey in 1916 and in New York shortly after, then soon began breeding in the wild. Over the years, Mute Swans have adapted well to the North American environment and have expanded their feral populations. Like many non-native species, Mute Swans are often fierce competitors for nesting areas and food sources. They can be very aggressive toward geese and ducks, often displacing many native species.

Other ID: all-white plumage. *Immature:* plumage may be white to grayish brown.
Size: *L* 5 ft; *W* 6¼ ft.
Voice: generally silent; may hiss or issue hoarse barking notes; loud wingbeats can be heard from up to a ½ mile away.
Status: common across the northern third of the state; less common southward.
Habitat: freshwater marshes, lakes and ponds.

Similar Birds

Tundra Swan   Trumpeter Swan

wings are often
held in an arch
over the back
while swimming

neck is usually held
in an S-shape

bulbous, black
knob extending
from the forehead

orange bill
with a down-
turned tip

Nesting: on the ground along a shoreline; female builds a mound of vegetation (male may help gather material); pale green eggs are 4½ x 3 in; female incubates 5–10 eggs for about 36 days.

Did You Know?

Weighing in at 35 pounds, as much as an average 4-year-old child, this large swan is one of the continent's heaviest flying birds.

Look For

Adult Mute Swans may be distinguished from our native swans by their orange bill with a black basal knob, S-shaped neck and a slightly longer tail.

Wood Duck

Aix sponsa

A forest-dwelling duck, the Wood Duck is equipped with fairly sharp claws for perching on branches and nesting in tree cavities. Shortly after hatching, the ducklings jump out of their nest cavity, often falling 20 feet or more. Like downy balls, they bounce on landing and are seldom injured. • Female Wood Ducks often return to the same nest site year after year, especially after successfully raising a brood. Established nest sites, where the adults are familiar with potential threats, may improve the young's chance of survival.

Other ID: *Male:* glossy green head with some white streaks; white-spotted, purplish chestnut breast; dark back and hindquarters.
Female: gray-brown upperparts; white belly.
Size: *L* 15–20 in; *W* 30 in.
Voice: *Male:* ascending *ter-wee-wee.*
Female: squeaky *woo-e-e-k.*
Status: common.
Habitat: swamps, ponds, marshes and lakeshores with wooded edges.

Similar Birds

Hooded Merganser
(p. 36)

Mallard
(p. 28)

head raised in flight ♂

white, teardrop-shaped eye patch

crest is slicked back from crown

♀

♂

mottled brown breast is streaked with white

golden sides

black and white shoulder slash

white chin and throat

Nesting: in a hollow or tree cavity; may be as high as 30 ft up; also in an artificial nest box; usually near water; cavity is lined with down; white to buff eggs are 2⅛ x 1⅝ in; female incubates 9–14 eggs for 25–35 days.

Did You Know?

The scientific name *sponsa* is Latin for "promised bride," suggesting that the male appears formally dressed for a wedding.

Look For

Landowners with a suitable wetland on their property may attract a family of Wood Ducks by erecting a nest box at a height of at least 5 feet and close to the shoreline.

Mallard
Anas platyrhynchos

The Mallard is Indiana's most common duck species and can be seen year-round. It is often found in flocks and is always near open water. This confident duck has even been spotted dabbling in outdoor swimming pools. In Indiana, it is most common during migration and winter, but it breeds in small numbers in the northwest corner of the state. • After breeding, male ducks lose their elaborate plumage, helping them stay camouflaged during their flightless period. In early fall, they molt back into breeding colors.

Other ID: orange feet. *Male:* white "necklace"; black tail feathers curl upward. *Female:* mottled brown overall.
Size: *L* 20–28 in; *W* 3 ft.
Voice: quacks; female is louder than male.
Status: abundant.
Habitat: lakes, wetlands, rivers, city parks, agricultural areas and sewage lagoons.

Similar Birds

Northern Shoveler   American Black Duck   Common Merganser

glossy, green head

orange bill
is spattered
with black

yellow bill

♂

♀

Nesting: a grass nest is built on the ground or under a bush; creamy, grayish or greenish white eggs are 2¼ x 1⅝ in; female incubates 7–10 eggs for 26–30 days.

Did You Know?

A nesting hen generates enough body heat to make the grass around her nest grow faster. She uses the tall grass to further conceal her nest.

Look For

Mallards will freely hybridize with American Black Ducks or domestic ducks, often producing offspring with very peculiar plumages.

Blue-winged Teal
Anas discors

Small, speedy Blue-winged Teals are renowned for their aviation skills. They are known for their small size and for the sharp twists and turns they execute in flight. • Blue-winged Teals and other dabbling ducks feed by tipping up their tails and dunking their heads underwater. Dabbling ducks have small feet situated near the center of their bodies. Other ducks, such as scoters, scaup and Buffleheads, dive underwater to feed, propelled by large feet set farther back on their bodies.

Other ID: broad, flat bill. *Female:* mottled brown overall. *In flight:* blue forewing patch; green speculum.
Size: *L* 14–16 in; *W* 23 in.
Voice: *Male:* soft *keck-keck-keck. Female:* soft quacks.
Status: common.
Habitat: shallow lake edges and wetlands; prefers areas with short but dense emergent vegetation.

Similar Birds

Green-winged Teal   Northern Shoveler

white throat

white crescent on face

blue-gray head

black-spotted breast and sides

Nesting: most often nests in the northern half of Indiana; along a grassy shoreline or in a meadow; nest is built with grass and considerable amounts of down; whitish eggs are 1¾ x 1¼ in; female incubates 8–13 eggs for 23–27 days.

Did You Know?

Compared to other ducks, the Blue-winged Teal is among the latest spring and earliest fall migrants.

Look For

Male Blue-winged Teals have a white crescent patch next to their bill that is visible year-round.

Lesser Scaup
Aythya affinis

Two scaup species occur in Indiana, and their tricolor appearance makes them easy to recognize and remember. The common Lesser Scaup has a smaller, white inner wing stripe that changes to dull gray on the primaries, while the rarer Greater Scaup has a larger, white wing stripe that extends into the primary flight feathers. Look for these field marks when the birds are in flight or stretching their wings on the water. The male Lesser Scaup also has a purple, peaked head while the Greater Scaup has a green, rounded head.

Other ID: gray-blue bill; white wing stripe; highest point of head is above and behind eye. *Male:* "black at both ends and light in the middle"; white, dark-tipped side feathers; grayish back; yellow eyes. *Female:* dark brown; white area encircles base of bill.

Size: L 15–18 in; W 25 in.

Voice: generally silent in winter; alarm call is a deep *scaup*. *Male:* soft *whee-oooh* in courtship. *Female:* purring *kwah*.

Status: common during migration and in winter.

Habitat: lakes, open marshes and along slow-moving rivers.

Similar Birds

Ring-necked Duck

Redhead

Greater Scaup

small, white wing patch

gray primaries

dark brown head with a white patch at base of bill

tall, compressed, purplish black head

♂

♀

Nesting: does not nest in Indiana; nests in Canada and the north-central U.S.; nest is in tall, concealing vegetation, generally close to water; nest hollow is built of grass and lined with down; pale olive or greenish eggs are 2¼ x 1½ in; female incubates 8–10 eggs for about 25 days.

Did You Know?

"Scaup" might be a phonetic imitation of this bird's call.

Look For

A member of the *Aythya* genus of diving ducks, the Lesser Scaup leaps up neatly before diving underwater, where it propels itself with powerful strokes of its feet.

Common Goldeneye
Bucephala clangula

The Common Goldeneye typically spends its entire life in North America, between its breeding grounds in the boreal forests of Canada and Alaska and its winter territory in marine bays and estuaries along the Atlantic and Pacific coasts. Many goldeneyes also overwinter on large inland rivers, lakes and reservoirs, depending on food availability and open water. • Fish, crustaceans and mollusks make up a major portion of the Common Goldeneye's winter diet.

Other ID: golden eyes. *Male:* dark, iridescent green head; dark back; white sides and belly. *Female:* lighter breast and belly; gray-brown body plumage; dark bill has yellow tip in spring and summer. *In flight:* extensive white on inner wing.
Size: L 16–20 in; W 26 in.
Voice: generally silent in migration and winter. *Male:* courtship calls are a nasal *peent* and a hoarse *kraaagh. Female:* a harsh croak.
Status: common in migration and winter.
Habitat: open water of lakes, large ponds and rivers.

Similar Birds

Bufflehead

Hooded Merganser
(p. 36)

black wings with large, white wing patches ♂

♀

chocolate brown head ♀

steep forehead with peaked crown

white, oval cheek patch

dark bill ♂

Nesting: does not nest in Indiana; nests in Canada and Alaska; in a tree cavity or occasionally a nest box lined with wood chips and down; often close to water; blue-green eggs are 2⅜ x 1⅝ in; female incubates 6–10 eggs for 28–32 days.

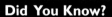

Did You Know?

In winter, female Common Goldeneyes fly farther south than males, and juvenile birds continue even farther south than adults.

Look For

Common Goldeneyes are frequently called "Whistlers," because the wind whistles through their wings when they fly.

Hooded Merganser
Lophodytes cucullatus

Extremely attractive and exceptionally shy, the male Hooded Merganser is one of the most sought-after ducks from a birder's perspective. Much of the time the drake's crest is held flat, but in moments of arousal or agitation he quickly unfolds his brilliant crest to attract a mate or to signal approaching danger. The drake displays his full range of colors and athletic abilities in elaborate, late-winter courtship displays and chases.
• Unusually, female Hooded Mergansers have been known to share incubation of eggs with female Wood Ducks and goldeneyes.

Other ID: *Male:* black head and back; bold, white crest is outlined in black; rusty sides. *Female:* dusky brown body; shaggy, reddish brown crest. *In flight:* small, white wing patches; white belly.
Size: *L* 16–18 in; *W* 24 in.
Voice: low grunts and croaks. *Male:* froglike *crrrrooo* in courtship display. *Female:* occasionally a harsh *gak* or a croaking *croo-croo-crook*.
Status: common.
Habitat: forest-edged ponds, wetlands, lakes and rivers.

Similar Birds

Wood Duck
(p. 26)

Bufflehead

Common Merganser

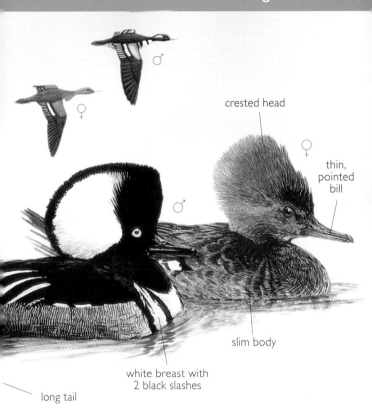

crested head

♀

thin,
pointed
bill

♂

slim body

white breast with
2 black slashes

long tail

Nesting: usually in a tree cavity lined with
leaves and down; white eggs are 2¼ x 1¾ in;
female incubates 10–12 eggs for 29–33 days.

Did You Know?

All mergansers have ser-
rated bills for grasping
slippery fish. The Hooded
Merganser also adds crus-
taceans, insects and
acorns to its diet.

Look For

The Hooded Merganser has
a long tail that is often held
erect while swimming.

Wild Turkey
Meleagris gallopavo

This charismatic bird is the only native North American animal that has been widely domesticated. The wild ancestors of most domestic animals came from Europe. • Early in life both male and female turkeys gobble. The females eventually outgrow this practice, leaving the males to gobble competitively for the honor of mating. • If Congress had taken Benjamin Franklin's advice in 1782, our national emblem would be the Wild Turkey instead of the Bald Eagle.

Other ID: large size; dark, glossy, iridescent body plumage; largely unfeathered legs. *Male:* red wattles, black-tipped breast feathers. *Female:* smaller; blue-gray head; less iridescent body; brown-tipped breast feathers.
Size: *Male:* L 3–3½ ft; W 5½ ft. *Female:* L 3 ft; W 4 ft.
Voice: courting male gobbles loudly; alarm call is a loud *pert*; gathering call is a cluck; contact call is a loud *keouk-keouk-keouk*.
Status: common and increasing.
Habitat: deciduous, mixed and riparian woodlands; occasionally visits fields in late fall and winter to eat waste grain and corn.

Similar Birds

Ring-necked Pheasant

Look For

Eastern Wild Turkeys have brown or rusty tail tips and are slimmer than domestic turkeys, which have white tail tips.

naked, blue-red head

barred, copper-colored tail

♂

long central breast tassel

Nesting: in a woodland or at a field edge; nests in a depression on the ground under thick cover; nest is lined with grass and leaves; brown-speckled, pale buff eggs are 2½ x 1¾ in; female incubates 10–12 eggs for up to 28 days.

Did You Know?

The Wild Turkey was once common throughout most of eastern North America, but in the early 20th century, habitat loss and overhunting took a toll on this bird. Today, efforts at restoration have reestablished the Wild Turkey throughout most of Indiana.

Northern Bobwhite
Colinus virginianus

The characteristic, whistled *bob-white* call of our only native quail is heard throughout Indiana in spring. The male's well-known call is often the only evidence of this bird's presence among the dense, tangled vegetation of its rural, woodland home. • In fall and winter, Northern Bobwhites typically travel in large family groups called coveys. When a predator approaches, the covey bursts into flight, creating a confusing flurry of activity. With the arrival of spring, breeding pairs break away from their coveys to perform elaborate courtship rituals in preparation for another nesting season.

Other ID: upperparts mottled with brown, buff and black; white crescents and spots edged in black on chestnut brown sides and upper breast; short tail.
Size: *L* 10 in; *W* 13 in.
Voice: whistled *hoy* is given year-round.
Male: a whistled, rising *bob-white* in spring and summer.
Status: uncommon and declining.
Habitat: farmlands, open woodlands, woodland edges, grassy fencelines, roadside ditches and brushy, open country.

Similar Birds

Ruffed Grouse

Look For

Bobwhites benefit from habitat disturbance and are often found in the early succession habitats created by fire, agriculture and forestry.

buff throat and
eyebrow

broad, white
eyebrow

♂

♀

white throat

rufous breast

Nesting: in a shallow depression on the
ground, often concealed by vegetation or
a woven, partial dome; nest is lined with grass
and leaves; white to pale buff eggs are 1¼ x 1 in;
pair incubates 12–16 eggs for 22–24 days.

Did You Know?

Northern Bobwhites may live as long as 6 years, but because
of high predation and other factors, about 80 percent of the
population doesn't make it past one year old. To make up for
this high mortality rate, Northern Bobwhites produce large
clutches of eggs—a single female may produce as many as
25 eggs in a year, if the season permits a second nesting.

Pied-billed Grebe
Podilymbus podiceps

Relatively solid bones and the ability to partially deflate its air sac allows the Pied-billed Grebe to sink below the surface of the water like a tiny submarine. This inconspicuous grebe can float low in the water or submerge with only its nostrils and eyes showing above the surface. • Pied-billed Grebes remain in Indiana during mild winters, but they are most common in migration, especially in fall, when flocks are often seen on large lakes.

Other ID: laterally compressed bill. *Breeding:* white undertail coverts; pale belly. *Nonbreeding:* bill lacks black ring; white chin and throat; brownish crown.
Size: L 12–15 in; W 16 in.
Voice: loud, whooping call begins quickly, then slows down: *kuk-kuk-kuk cow cow cow cowp cowp cowp.*
Status: common and widespread.
Habitat: ponds, marshes and backwaters with sparse emergent vegetation.

Similar Birds

American Coot
(p. 70)

Horned Grebe

dark eye with pale eye ring

black throat

all-brown body

black ring on pale, thick bill

breeding

very short tail

Nesting: among sparse vegetation in wetlands; floating platform nest, made of decaying plants, is anchored to emergent vegetation; white to buff eggs are 1⅝ x 1¼ in; pair incubates 4–5 eggs for about 23 days.

Did You Know?

When frightened by an intruder, this grebe will cover its eggs and slide underwater, leaving a nest that looks like nothing more than a mat of debris.

Look For

Dark plumage, individually webbed toes and a chicken-like bill distinguish the Pied-billed Grebe from other waterfowl.

Double-crested Cormorant
Phalacrocorax auritus

The Double-crested Cormorant looks like a bird but smells and swims like a fish. With a long, rudderlike tail and excellent underwater vision, this slick-feathered bird has mastered the underwater world. Most waterbirds have waterproof feathers, but the Double-crested Cormorant's feathers allow water in. "Wettable" feathers make this bird less buoyant, which in turn makes it a better diver. The Double-crested Cormorant also has sealed nostrils for diving, and therefore must fly with its bill open.

Other ID: all-black body; blue eyes.
Immature: brown upperparts; buff throat and breast; yellowish throat patch. *In flight:* rapid wingbeats; kinked neck.
Size: *L* 26–32 in; *W* 4¼ ft.
Voice: generally quiet; may issue piglike grunts or croaks, especially near nest colonies.
Status: abundant and increasing.
Habitat: large lakes and large, meandering rivers.

Similar Birds

Common Loon

Look For

These birds often perch on trees or piers with their wings partially spread. Lacking oil glands, they use the wind to dry their feathers.

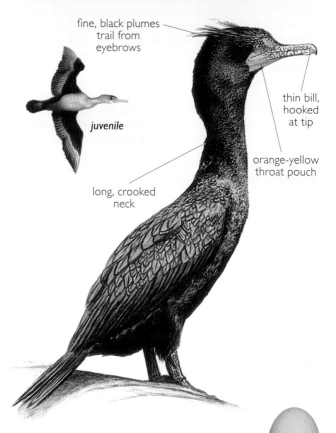

fine, black plumes trail from eyebrows

thin bill, hooked at tip

juvenile

orange-yellow throat pouch

long, crooked neck

Nesting: colonial; on an island or high in a tree; platform nest is made of sticks and guano; pale blue eggs are 2 x 1½ in; pair incubates 2–7 eggs for 25–30 days.

Did You Know?

Fish make up a large part of the Double-crested Cormorant's diet, and it was once believed that this bird competed with commercial and recreational fishermen. However, in natural environments, cormorants generally take undesirable species, such as alewifes, smelts and yellow perch.

Great Blue Heron
Ardea herodias

The long-legged Great Blue Heron has a stealthy, often motionless hunting strategy. It waits for a fish or frog to approach, spears the prey with its bill, then flips its catch into the air and swallows it whole. Herons usually hunt near water, but they also stalk fields and meadows in search of rodents. • Great Blue Herons settle in communal treetop nests called rookeries. Nesting herons are sensitive to human disturbance, so observe this bird's behavior from a distance.

Other ID: blue-gray overall; long, dark legs. *Breeding:* richer colors; plumes streak from crown and throat. *In flight:* black upperwing tips; legs trail behind body; slow, steady wingbeats; head not extended.
Size: L 4¼–4½ ft; W 6 ft.
Voice: quiet away from the nest; occasional harsh *frahnk frahnk frahnk* during takeoff.
Status: common and increasing.
Habitat: forages along edges of rivers, lakes and marshes; also in fields and wet meadows.

Similar Birds

Little Blue Heron

Great Egret
(p. 48)

Sandhill Crane
(p. 72)

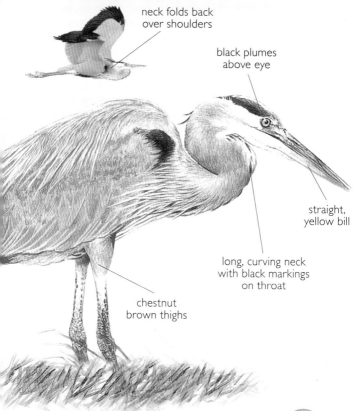

neck folds back
over shoulders

black plumes
above eye

straight,
yellow bill

long, curving neck
with black markings
on throat

chestnut
brown thighs

Nesting: colonial; adds to its stick platform nest over years; nest width can reach 4 ft; pale bluish green eggs are 2½ x 1¾ in; pair incubates 4–7 eggs for approximately 28 days.

Did You Know?

The Great Blue Heron is the tallest of all herons and egrets in North America.

Look For

In flight, the Great Blue Heron folds its neck back over its shoulders in an S-shape. Similar-looking cranes stretch their necks out when flying.

Great Egret
Ardea alba

The plumes of Great Egrets and Snowy Egrets were widely used to decorate hats in the early 20th century. An ounce of egret feathers cost as much as $32—more than an ounce of gold at that time—and, as a result, egret populations began to disappear. Some of the first conservation legislation in North America was enacted to outlaw the hunting of Great Egrets. The Great Egret is the symbol for the National Audubon Society, one of the oldest conservation organizations in the United States.• These beautiful birds are widespread throughout the state in August and September.

Other ID: all-white plumage. *In flight:* neck folds back over shoulders; black legs extend backward.
Size: L 3–3½ ft; W 4 ft.
Voice: rapid, low-pitched, loud *cuk-cuk-cuk*.
Status: common migrant; a species of special concern as a breeding species.
Habitat: marshes, open riverbanks, irrigation canals and lakeshores.

Similar Birds

Orange-crowned Warbler

American Goldfinch

Common Yellowthroat

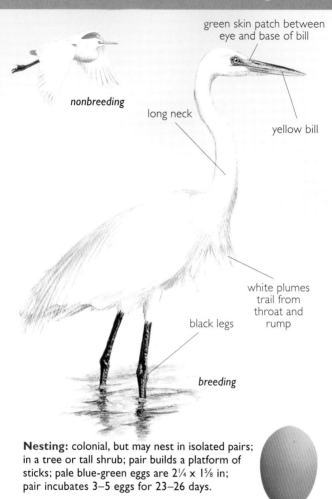

nonbreeding

green skin patch between eye and base of bill

long neck

yellow bill

white plumes trail from throat and rump

black legs

breeding

Nesting: colonial, but may nest in isolated pairs; in a tree or tall shrub; pair builds a platform of sticks; pale blue-green eggs are 2¼ x 1⅝ in; pair incubates 3–5 eggs for 23–26 days.

Did You Know?

The oldest Great Egret on record lived to 22 years old.

Look For

A crafty Great Egret will sometimes feed near a White Ibis, taking advantage of prey that the ibis frightens to the surface but cannot reach.

Green Heron
Butorides virescens

Sentinel of the marshes, the ever-vigilant Green Heron sits hunched on a shaded branch at the water's edge. This crow-sized heron stalks frogs and small fish lurking in the weedy shallows, then stabs the prey with its bill. • Unlike most herons, the Green Heron nests singly rather than communally, though it can sometimes be found in loose colonies. While some of this heron's habitat has been lost to wetland drainage or channelization in the southern states, the building of farm ponds or reservoirs has created habitat in other areas.

Other ID: small, stocky body; relatively short, yellow-green legs; bill is dark above and greenish below; short tail. *Breeding male:* bright orange legs. *Immature:* heavy streaking along neck and under-parts; dark brown upperparts.
Size: L 15–22 in; W 26 in.
Voice: generally silent; alarm and flight call are a loud *kowp, kyow* or *skow*; aggression call is a harsh *raah*.
Status: common.
Habitat: marshes, lakes and streams with dense shoreline or emergent vegetation, mangroves.

Similar Birds

Black-crowned
Night Heron

Least Bittern

American Bittern

dark, iridescent back

green-black
crown

chestnut face
and neck

Nesting: nests singly or in small, loose groups; platform nest in a tree or shrub, usually very close to water; pale blue-green eggs are 1½ x 1⅛ in; pair incubates 3–5 eggs for 19–21 days.

Did You Know?

In Asia, Green Herons have been seen baiting fish to the water's surface by dropping small bits of debris such as twigs, vegetation or feathers.

Look For

The Green Heron often appears bluish or black; the iridescent green shine on the back and outer wings is only visible in certain light.

Turkey Vulture
Cathartes aura

Turkey Vultures are intelligent, playful and social birds. Groups live and sleep together in large trees, or "roosts." Some roost sites are over a century old and have been used by the same family of vultures for several generations. • The genus name *Cathartes* means "cleanser" and refers to this bird's affinity for carrion. A vulture's bill and feet are much less powerful than those of eagles, hawks or falcons, which kill live prey. Its red, featherless head may appear grotesque, but this adaptation allows the bird to stay relatively clean while feeding on messy carcasses.

Other ID: *Immature:* dark gray head. *In flight:* head appears small; rocks from side to side when soaring; flight feathers are paler than rest of underwing.
Size: *L* 25–31 in; *W* 5½–6 ft.
Voice: generally silent; occasionally produces a hiss or grunt if threatened.
Status: common.
Habitat: usually flies over open country, shorelines or roads; rarely over forests.

Similar Birds

Bald Eagle
(p. 56)

Black Vulture

Golden Eagle

wings are held in a shallow "V"

silver gray flight feathers

bare, red head

brownish overall

pale, hooked bill

Nesting: in a cave, crevice, log or among boulders; uses no nest material; dull white or creamy, brown-spotted eggs are 2¾ x 2 in; pair incubates 2 eggs for up to 41 days.

Did You Know?

A threatened Turkey Vulture will play dead or throw up. The odor of its vomit repulses attackers, much like the odor of a skunk's spray.

Look For

No other bird uses updrafts and thermals in flight as well as the Turkey Vulture. Pilots have reported seeing vultures soaring at 20,000 feet.

Osprey
Pandion haliaetus

The large, powerful Osprey is almost always found near water. Its dark eye line blocks the glare of the sun on the water, enabling the bird to spot fish near the water's surface. While hunting, the Osprey hovers in the air before hurling itself in a dramatic headfirst dive. An instant before striking the water, it rights itself and thrusts its feet forward to grasp its quarry. The Osprey has specialized feet for gripping slippery prey—two toes point forward, two point backward and all are covered with sharp spines.

Other ID: yellow eyes; pale crown. *Male:* all-white throat. *Female:* fine, dark "necklace."
In flight: long wings are held in a shallow "M"; dark "wrist"
patches; brown and white tail bands.
Size: *L* 22–25 in; *W* 5½–6 ft.
Voice: series of melodious ascending whistles: *chewk-chewk-chewk*; also a familiar *kip-kip-kip*.
Status: endangered as a breeding species in Indiana, but uncommon as a migrant.
Habitat: lakes and slow-flowing rivers and streams; estuaries and bays in migration.

Similar Birds

Bald Eagle
(p. 56)

Rough-legged Hawk

dark eye line

gray bill

♂

gray feet

long wings
extend past tail

Nesting: on a treetop or artificial structure, usually near water; massive stick nest is reused annually; yellowish, brown-blotched eggs are 2⅜ x 1¾ in; pair incubates 2–4 eggs for 38 days.

Did You Know?

The Indiana Department of Natural Resources has implemented an Osprey reintroduction program.

Look For

Ospreys build bulky nests on high, artificial structures such as communication towers and utility poles, or on buoys and channel markers over water.

Bald Eagle

Haliaeetus leucocephalus

The Bald Eagle, a symbol of freedom, longevity and strength, became the emblem of the United States in 1782. This majestic sea eagle hunts mostly fish and is often found near water. While soaring hundreds of feet high in the air, an eagle can spot fish swimming underwater and small rodents scurrying through the grass. This eagle also scavenges carrion and steals food from other birds.
• Bald Eagles do not mature until their fourth or fifth year—only then do they develop the characteristic white head and tail plumage.

Other ID: *1st year:* dark overall; dark bill; some white in underwings. *2nd year:* dark "bib"; white in underwings. *3rd year:* mostly white plumage; yellow at base of bill; yellow eyes. *4th year:* light head with dark facial streak; variable pale and dark plumage; yellow bill; paler eyes.
Size: *L* 30–43 in; *W* 5½–8 ft.
Voice: thin, weak squeal or gull-like cackle, *kleek-kik-kik-kik* or *kah-kah-kah.*
Status: endangered, but prospering in the wake of a Department of Natural Resources reintroduction program.
Habitat: large lakes and rivers.

Similar Birds

Osprey
(p. 54)

Look For

In winter, hundreds of ducks will gather on industrial ponds or other ice-free waters, unknowingly providing an easy meal for hungry Bald Eagles.

white head
and tail

yellow bill

immature

yellow feet

Nesting: more than 50 active nests in the state; usually, but not always, near water; in a tree; huge stick nest is often reused for many years; white eggs are 2¾ x 2⅛ in; pair incubates 1–3 eggs for 34–36 days.

Did You Know?

Bald Eagles generally mate for life. A pair will renew bonds each year by adding new sticks and branches to its massive nest, the largest of any North American bird. If a pair needs to build a nest from scratch, the process can take as long as three months.

Northern Harrier
Circus cyaneus

With its prominent white rump and distinctive, slightly upturned wings, the Northern Harrier, formerly known as the "Marsh Hawk," may be the easiest raptor to identify in flight. Unlike other midsized birds, it often flies close to the ground, relying on sudden surprise attacks to capture prey. • The courtship flight of the Northern Harrier is a spectacle worth watching in spring. The male climbs almost vertically in the air, then stalls and plummets in a reckless dive toward the ground. At the last second he saves himself with a hairpin turn that sends him skyward again.

Other ID: *Male:* bluish gray to silver gray upperparts; white underparts; indistinct tail bands, except for 1 dark subterminal band. *Female:* dark brown upperparts; streaky, brown and buff underparts. *In flight:* long, slender wings and tail; black wing tips; white rump.
Size: L 16–24 in; W 3½–4 ft.
Voice: generally quiet; high-pitched *ke-ke-ke-ke-ke-ke* near the nest or during courtship.
Status: endangered as a breeding species, but otherwise fairly common.
Habitat: open country, including fields, wet meadows, cattail marshes, bogs and croplands.

Similar Birds

Red-tailed Hawk
(p. 62)

Broad-winged Hawk

Red-shouldered
Hawk

facial disc

♀

♀

♂

yellow legs

long, dark-banded tail

Nesting: on the ground; usually in tall vegetation or on a raised mound; shallow depression is lined with grass, sticks and cattails; bluish white eggs are 1⅞ x 1⅜ in; female incubates 4–6 eggs for 30–32 days.

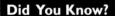

Did You Know?

Britain's Royal Air Force was so impressed by the Northern Harrier's maneuverability that it named the Harrier aircraft after this bird.

Look For

The Northern Harrier has an owl-like, parabolic facial disc. As with the owls, this structure enhances the harrier's hearing, allowing it to hunt by sound as well as by sight.

Cooper's Hawk
Accipiter cooperii

A Cooper's Hawk will quickly scatter songbirds at a backyard bird feeder when it comes looking for a meal. European Starlings, American Robins and House Sparrows are among its favorite choices of prey. • You might also spot this songbird scavenger hunting along forest edges. With the help of its short, square tail and flap-and-glide flight, it is capable of maneuvering quickly at high speeds to snatch its prey in midair. • Female birds of prey are always larger than the males. The female Cooper's Hawk does not hesitate to hunt birds as large as a Rock Pigeon.

Other ID: crow-sized bird; short, rounded wings; dark barring on pale undertail and underwings; blue-gray back; white terminal tail band.
Size: *Male: L* 15–17 in; *W* 27–32 in.
Female: L 17–19 in; *W* 32–37 in.
Voice: fast, woodpecker-like *cac-cac-cac-cac.*
Status: common and increasing.
Habitat: mixed woodlands, riparian woodlands, urban gardens with feeders.

Similar Birds

Sharp-shinned Hawk

Merlin

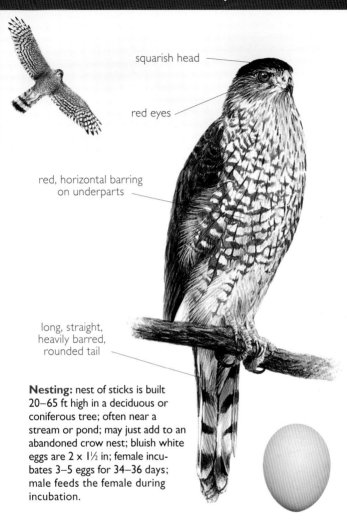

squarish head

red eyes

red, horizontal barring on underparts

long, straight, heavily barred, rounded tail

Nesting: nest of sticks is built 20–65 ft high in a deciduous or coniferous tree; often near a stream or pond; may just add to an abandoned crow nest; bluish white eggs are 2 x 1½ in; female incubates 3–5 eggs for 34–36 days; male feeds the female during incubation.

Did You Know?

Cooper's Hawks have adapted to nesting in suburban trees, which greatly expands their available breeding habitat.

Look For

The Cooper's Hawk is slightly larger and has a more rounded tail tip than the similar looking Sharp-shinned Hawk, which also occurs in Indiana.

Red-tailed Hawk

Buteo jamaicensis

Take an afternoon drive through the country and look for Red-tailed Hawks soaring above the fields. Red-tails are the most common hawks in Indiana, especially during migration. • In warm weather, these hawks use thermals and updrafts to soar. The pockets of rising air provide substantial lift, which allows migrating hawks to fly for almost 2 miles without flapping their wings. On cooler days, resident Red-tails perch on exposed tree limbs, fence posts or utility poles to scan for prey. • The Red-tailed Hawk's piercing call is often paired with the image of an eagle in TV commercials and movies.

Other ID: brown eyes. *In flight:* light under-wing flight feathers with faint barring; dark leading edge on underside of inner wing.
Size: *Male: L* 18–23 in; *W* 4–5 ft.
Female: L 20–25 in; *W* 4–5 ft.
Voice: powerful, descending scream: *keeearrrr.*
Status: common and widespread.
Habitat: open country with some trees; also roadsides or woodlots.

Similar Birds

Rough-legged Hawk

Broad-winged Hawk

Red-shouldered Hawk

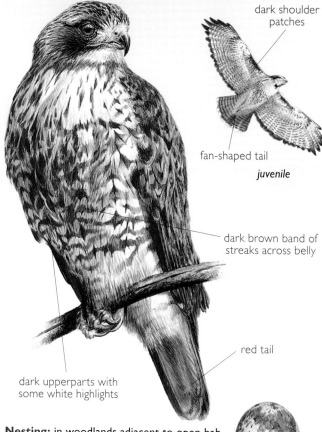

dark shoulder patches

fan-shaped tail

juvenile

dark brown band of streaks across belly

red tail

dark upperparts with some white highlights

Nesting: in woodlands adjacent to open habitat; bulky stick nest is enlarged each year; brown-blotched, whitish eggs are 2⅜ x 1⅞ in; pair incubates 2–4 eggs for 28–35 days.

Did You Know?

Courting birds will dive at one another, lock talons and tumble toward the earth, breaking away at the last second to avoid crashing into the ground.

Look For

Red-tailed Hawks often forage in the short vegetation found along margins of interstate highways.

American Kestrel
Falco sparverius

The colorful American Kestrel, formerly known as the "Sparrow Hawk," is a common and widespread falcon, not shy of human activity and adaptable to habitat change. This small falcon has benefited from the grassy rights-of-way created by interstate highways, which provide habitat for grasshoppers and other small prey. Watch for this robin-sized bird along rural roadways, perched on poles and telephone wires or hovering over agricultural fields, foraging for insects and small mammals.

Other ID: lightly spotted underparts. *Male:* blue-gray crown with rusty cap. *In flight:* pointed wings; frequently hovers; buoyant, indirect flight style.
Size: L 7½–8 in; W 20–24 in.
Voice: usually silent; loud, often repeated, shrill *killy-killy-killy* when excited; female's voice is lower pitched.
Status: common.
Habitat: open fields, riparian woodlands, woodlots, forest edges, bogs, roadside ditches, grassy highway medians, grasslands and croplands.

Similar Birds

Merlin

Sharp-shinned Hawk

Peregrine Falcon
(p. 66)

long, rusty tail ♀

2 distinctive facial stripes

rusty barring on back

♀

blue-gray wings

♂

Nesting: in a tree cavity; may use a nest box; white to buff, brown-spotted eggs are 1½ x 1⅛ in; mostly the female incubates 4–6 eggs for 29–30 days; pair raises the young together.

Did You Know?

No stranger to captivity, the American Kestrel was the first falcon to reproduce by artificial insemination.

Look For

While scouting for prey from a perch, the American Kestrel repeatedly lifts and lowers its tail.

Peregrine Falcon
Falco peregrinus

Nothing causes more panic in a flock of ducks or shorebirds than a hunting Peregrine Falcon. This powerful raptor matches every twist and turn the flock makes, then dives to strike a lethal blow. The Peregrine Falcon is the world's fastest bird. In a headfirst dive, it can reach speeds of up to 220 miles per hour. • In spring and fall, the migratory "Tundra" race passes through our state. This subspecies has slightly paler gray upperparts and fewer markings on the breast and belly.

Other ID: blue-gray back; yellow feet and cere.
In flight: pointed wings; long, narrow, dark-banded tail.
Size: *Male: L* 15–17 in; *W* 3–3½ ft.
Female: L 17–19 in; *W* 3½–4 ft.
Voice: loud, harsh, continuous *cack-cack-cack-cack-cack* near the nest site.
Status: uncommon and local.
Habitat: lakeshores, river valleys, river mouths, urban areas and open fields.

Similar Birds

Merlin

Look For

A pair of peregrines will sometimes nest on the ledge of a tall building or even a steel mill, right in the middle of an urban area.

dark "helmet"

white to buff chin and throat

prominent, pale underparts with fine, dark spotting and flecking

Nesting: usually on a rocky cliff or cut-bank; may use a skyscraper or factory ledge; nest site is often reused and littered with prey remains; white eggs with reddish specks are 2 x 1½ in; pair incubates 3–5 eggs for 32–34 days.

Did You Know?

In the 1960s, the pesticide DDT caused Peregrines to lay eggs with thin shells that broke easily. Peregrine populations declined dramatically until DDT was banned in North America in 1972. Since then, hundreds of captive-bred peregrines have been successfully reintroduced to the wild.

Sora
Porzana carolina

Soras have small bodies and large, chickenlike feet. Even without webbed feet, these unique creatures swim quite well over short distances. • Two rising *or-Ah or-Ah* whistles followed by a strange, descending whinny indicate that a Sora is nearby. Although the Sora is the most common and widespread rail species in North America, it is seldom seen. This secretive bird prefers to remain hidden in dense marshland, but it will occasionally venture into the shallows to search for aquatic insects and mollusks.

Other ID: *Nonbreeding:* less black on face and throat. *Immature:* no black on face; bill is darker; paler underparts.
Size: *L* 8–10 in; *W* 14 in.
Voice: clear, 2-note *coo-wee*; alarm call is a sharp *keek;* courtship song begins *or-Ah or-Ah* followed by a maniacal, descending *weee-weee-weee.*
Status: Indiana's most common rail; more often heard than seen.
Habitat: wetlands with abundant emergent cattails, bulrushes, sedges and grasses.

Similar Birds

Virginia Rail   King Rail

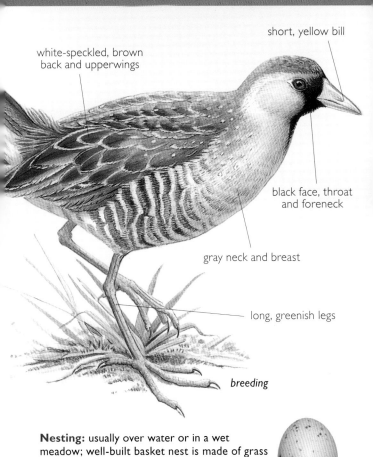

short, yellow bill

white-speckled, brown
back and upperwings

black face, throat
and foreneck

gray neck and breast

long, greenish legs

breeding

Nesting: usually over water or in a wet
meadow; well-built basket nest is made of grass
and aquatic vegetation; darkly speckled, buff or
olive buff eggs are 1¼ x ⅞ in; pair incubates
10–12 eggs for 18–20 days.

Did You Know?

Literally "as thin as a rail," the Sora has a very narrow body that allows it to squeeze through thick stands of cattails.

Look For

The Sora has long legs, a stumpy body and almost no neck. It bustles through the shallows, darting in and out of the reeds.

American Coot
Fulica americana

American Coots resemble ducks but are actually more closely related to rails and gallinules. The numbers of coots that breed in Indiana fluctuates yearly, but good numbers appear on our lakes, reservoirs and wetlands during migration in April and from October through November. • With feet that have individually webbed toes, the coot is well adapted for diving for its food. Nonetheless, it will sometimes steal a meal from another skilled diver.

Other ID: red eyes; long, yellow-green legs; lobed toes; small, white marks on tail.
Size: *L* 13–16 in; *W* 24 in.
Voice: calls frequently in summer, day and night: *kuk-kuk-kuk-kuk-kuk;* also croaks and grunts.
Status: common to abundant.
Habitat: shallow marshes, ponds and wetlands with open water and emergent vegetation; also sewage lagoons.

Similar Birds

Common Moorhen   Pied-billed Grebe
(p. 42)

reddish spot on
white forehead
shield

gray-black overall

white, chicken-
like bill with
dark ring
around tip

Nesting: in emergent vegetation; pair builds
a floating nest of cattails and grass; buffy white,
brown-spotted eggs are 2 x 1⅜ in; pair incubates 8–12 eggs for 21–25 days; often produces
2 broods per year.

Did You Know?

American Coots are the
most widespread and
abundant members of
the rail family in North
America.

Look For

Though it resembles a duck,
an American Coot bobs its
head while swimming or
walking and has a narrower
bill that extends up the forehead.

Sandhill Crane
Grus canadensis

The Sandhill Crane's deep, rattling call can be heard long before this bird passes overhead. Its coiled trachea alters the pitch of its voice, making its call sound louder and carry farther. At first glance, large, V-shaped flocks of Sandhill Cranes look like flocks of Canada Geese, but the cranes often soar and circle in the air, and they do not honk like geese. • Cranes mate for life and reinforce pair bonds each spring with an elaborate courtship dance. The ritual looks much like human dancing, which may seem a strange comparison until you witness the spectacle firsthand. • Look for these birds in cornfields along river valleys.

Other ID: large bird; long, straight bill; long neck; dark legs.
Size: L 3¼–4¼ ft; W 6–7 ft.
Voice: loud, resonant, rattling: *gu-rrroo gu-rrroo gurrroo.*
Status: species of special concern as a breeder; otherwise abundant.
Habitat: agricultural fields and shorelines.

Similar Birds

Great Blue Heron
(p. 46)

Whooping Crane

naked, red crown

white cheek
and chin

gray plumage is often
stained rusty red from
iron oxides in the water

Nesting: rarely nests in Indiana, but breeding
birds are increasing; nests in Canada, Alaska and
locally in the northern U.S.; in the water or along
the shoreline; on a large mound of aquatic vegetation; brown-blotched, buff eggs are 3¾ x 2⅜ in;
pair incubates 2 eggs for 29–32 days.

Did You Know?

Flocks of migrating
Sandhill Cranes are usually
made up of close family
members.

Look For

During migration, Sandhill
Cranes gather at Jasper-
Pulaski Fish and Wildlife Area
to refuel. The greatest num-
bers occur in March and
November.

Killdeer
Charadrius vociferus

The Killdeer is a gifted actor, well known for its "broken wing" distraction display. When an intruder wanders too close to its nest, the Killdeer greets the interloper with piteous cries while dragging a wing and stumbling about as if injured. Most predators take the bait and follow, and once the Killdeer has lured the predator far away from its nest, it miraculously recovers from the injury and flies off with a loud call.

Other ID: brown head; 2 black breast bands; brown back and upperwings; white underparts; rufous rump.
Size: *L* 9–11 in; *W* 24 in.
Voice: loud, distinctive *kill-dee kill-dee kill-deer;* variations include *deer-deer.*
Status: very common and widespread.
Habitat: open areas, such as fields, lakeshores, sandy beaches, mudflats, gravel streambeds, wet meadows and grasslands.

Similar Birds

Semipalmated Plover

Piping Plover

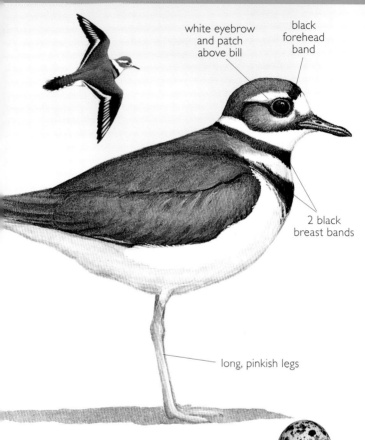

white eyebrow and patch above bill

black forehead band

2 black breast bands

long, pinkish legs

Nesting: on open ground; in a shallow, usually unlined depression; heavily marked, creamy buff eggs are 1⅜ x 1⅛ in; pair incubates 4 eggs for 24–28 days; may raise 2 broods.

Did You Know?

In spring, you might hear a European Starling imitate the vocal Killdeer's call.

Look For

The Killdeer has adapted well to urbanization, and it finds golf courses, farms, fields and abandoned industrial areas as much to its liking as shore-lines.

Lesser Yellowlegs
Tringa flavipes

The "tattletale" Lesser Yellowlegs is the self-appointed sentinel in a mixed flock of shorebirds, raising the alarm at the first sign of a threat. • It is challenging to discern Lesser Yellowlegs and Greater Yellowlegs (*T. melanoleuca*) in the field, but with practice, you will notice that the Lesser's bill is finer, straighter and shorter—about as long as its head is wide. With its long legs and wings, the Lesser appears slimmer and taller than the Greater, and it is more commonly seen in flocks. Finally, the Lesser Yellowlegs emits a pair of peeps, while the Greater Yellowlegs peeps three times in a row.

Other ID: subtle, dark eye line; pale lores. *Nonbreeding:* grayer overall.
Size: L 10–11 in; W 24 in.
Voice: typically a high-pitched pair of *tew* notes; noisiest on breeding grounds.
Status: very common during migration.
Habitat: shorelines of lakes, rivers, marshes and ponds.

Similar Birds

Greater Yellowlegs

Willet

Solitary Sandpiper

nonbreeding

brown-black mottling
on upperparts

all-dark bill is
not noticeably
longer than
width of head

no barring on belly

bright yellow legs

breeding

Nesting: does not nest in Indiana; nests in Canada and the Arctic; in open muskeg or a natural forest opening; in a depression on a dry mound lined with leaves and grass; darkly blotched, buff to olive eggs are 1⅝ x 1⅛ in; pair incubates 4 eggs for 22–23 days.

Did You Know?

In Indiana, the Lesser Yellowlegs is considerably more common than its larger cousin, the Greater Yellowlegs.

Look For

When feeding, the Lesser Yellowlegs wades into water almost to its belly, sweeping its bill back and forth just below the water's surface.

Sanderling
Calidris alba

This lucky shorebird graces sandy shorelines around the world. The Sanderling chases the waves in and out, snatching up aquatic invertebrates before they are swept back into the water. On shores where wave action is limited, it resorts to probing mudflats for a meal of mollusks and insects. • To keep warm, Sanderlings seek the company of roosting sandpipers or plovers and turnstones. They will also take a rest from their zigzag dance along a beach to stand with one leg tucked up, a posture that conserves body heat.

Other ID: *Nonbreeding:* pale gray upperparts; black shoulder patch (often concealed). *In flight:* dark leading edge of wing; broad, white stripe across upperwing.
Size: L 7–8½ in; W 17 in.
Voice: flight call is a sharp *kip* or *plick*.
Status: common from late July through mid-October on Lake Michigan beaches; rare inland.
Habitat: sandy and muddy shorelines, cobble and pebble beaches, spits, lakeshores, marshes and reservoirs.

Similar Birds

Dunlin

Least Sandpiper

Semipalmated Sandpiper

breeding

dark mottling on
rufous head, breast
and upperparts

relatively
short, black
bill

white underparts

breeding

Nesting: does not nest in Indiana; nests in the
Arctic; on the ground; cup nest is lined with
leaves; olive eggs, blotched with brown or purple, are 1½ x 1 in; pair incubates 3–4 eggs for
23–24 days.

Did You Know?

The Sanderling is wide-
spread, breeding across
the Arctic and wintering
on whatever continent it
chooses, excluding
Antarctica.

Look For

Sanderlings in pale nonbreeding plumage reflect a ghostly
glow as they forage at night
on moonlit beaches.

Pectoral Sandpiper
Calidris melanotos

The Pectoral Sandpiper is Indiana's most common shorebird. It gets its name from the location of the male's prominent air sacs. When displaying on his arctic breeding grounds, the male will inflate these air sacs, causing his breast feathers to rise. During displays, the male also emits a hollow hooting sound that has been likened to the sound of a foghorn. • This widespread traveler has been observed in every state and province in North America during its epic annual migrations. In spring and fall, large flocks of hundreds or even thousands of Pectoral Sandpipers are conspicuous in wet, grassy fields and along shorelines.

Other ID: white undertail coverts; black bill has slightly downcurved tip; mottled upperparts; may have faintly rusty, dark crown and back; folded wings extend beyond tail.
Size: *L* 9 in; *W* 18 in. (female is noticeably smaller)
Voice: sharp, short, low *krrick krrick*.
Status: abundant during migration.
Habitat: lakeshores, marshes, mudflats and flooded fields or pastures.

Similar Birds

Semipalmated
Sandpiper

Least Sandpiper

brown breast streaks end abruptly at edge of white belly

long, yellow legs

Nesting: does not nest in Indiana; nests in the Arctic; on flat, wet tundra with grass-sedge cover; in a shallow depression lined with grass; brown-blotched, pale olive eggs are 1½ x 1 in; female incubates 4 eggs for 21–23 days.

Did You Know?

Fall migration for the Pectoral Sandpiper begins in early July, as is the case with many shorebirds.

Look For

Unlike most sandpipers, the Pectoral exhibits sexual dimorphism—the female is only two-thirds the size of the male.

American Woodcock
Scolopax minor

The American Woodcock is a solitary shorebird that lives in moist woodlands, avoids saline habitats and remains hidden during daylight hours. • During the breeding season, the male American Woodcock performs a dazzling courtship display. At dawn or dusk, he struts around while uttering a series of loud *peent* notes. He then launches into the air in a circular flight until, with wings partly folded, he plummets to the ground in a zigzag pattern, chirping at every turn and returns to where he started. Twittering sounds are made by air rushing past the outer primary flight feathers.

Other ID: very long bill; stocky body with boldly patterned upperparts. *In flight:* rounded wings make a whistling sound (similar to Mourning Dove).
Size: *L* 11 in; *W* 18 in.
Voice: call is a nasal *peent*.
Status: common.
Habitat: moist woodlands and hammocks adjacent to grassy clearings or fields.

Similar Birds

Wilson's Snipe

Short-billed Dowitcher

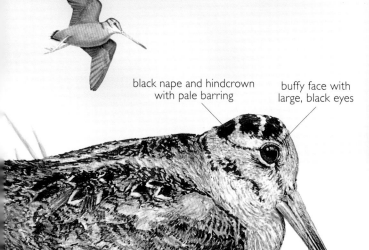

black nape and hindcrown with pale barring

buffy face with large, black eyes

long, mainly pale, straight bill

pale orange underparts

Nesting: on the ground; female digs a scrape and lines it with dried leaves; brown-blotched, creamy buff eggs are 1½ x 1¼ in; female incubates 4 eggs for 20–22 days and tends the young.

Did You Know?

The clearing of forests and draining of woodland swamps has degraded large tracts of woodcock habitat, resulting in population declines.

Look For

Watch for woodcocks at twilight from late February through April, when males perform their aerial courtship display over overgrown fields.

Bonaparte's Gull
Larus philadelphia

This gull's jet black head gives it an appealing elegance. With its delicate plumage and behavior, the small Bonaparte's Gull is nothing like its brash relatives. It avoids landfills, preferring to dine on insects caught in midair or plucked from the water's surface. The Bonaparte's Gull raises its soft, scratchy voice in excitement only when it spies a school of fish or an intruder near its nest. • The phrase "black-bill Bonaparte's" is a useful memory aid for identification.

Other ID: *Nonbreeding:* white head; dark ear patch. *In flight:* buoyant in the air; white forewing wedge; black wing tips.
Size: *L* 12–14 in; *W* 33 in.
Voice: scratchy, soft *ear ear* while feeding.
Status: common migrant.
Habitat: large lakes, rivers and marine nearshore upwellings.

Similar Birds

Franklin's Gull

Ring-billed Gull
(p. 86)

Laughing Gull

white eye ring

black head

nonbreeding

gray mantle

black bill

white underparts

orange legs

breeding

Nesting: does not nest in Indiana; nests in the northern Great Plains and Canadian Prairies; occasionally in large colonies; builds a deep nest bowl on the short, thick branches of a conifer; brown-blotched, olive to buff eggs are 2 x 1⅜ in; pair incubates 2–3 eggs for 24 days.

Did You Know?

This gull was named after Charles-Lucien Bonaparte, nephew of Napoleon Bonaparte, a naturalist who did ornithological research in the 1800s.

Look For

The Bonaparte's Gull has a light, buoyant flight and in migration large flocks can be spotted plucking food from the water's surface.

Ring-billed Gull

Larus delawarensis

Few people can claim that they have never seen this common, widespread gull. Highly tolerant of humans, the Ring-billed Gull is part of our every-day lives, scavenging our litter and frequenting our parks. This omnivorous gull eats almost anything and swarms parks, beaches, golf courses and fast-food parking lots looking for handouts, making a pest of itself. However, few species have adjusted to human development as well as the Ring-billed Gull, which is something to appreciate.

Other ID: yellow bill; pale gray mantle; yellow eyes; white underparts. *In flight:* black wing tips with a few white spots.
Size: L 18–20 in; W 4 ft.
Voice: high-pitched *kakakaka-akakaka*; also a low, laughing *yook-yook-yook*.
Status: abundant.
Habitat: *Breeding:* bare, rocky and shrubby islands and sewage ponds. *In migration* and *winter:* lakes, rivers, landfills, golf courses, parking lots, fields and parks.

Similar Birds

Herring Gull
(p. 88)

Glaucous Gull

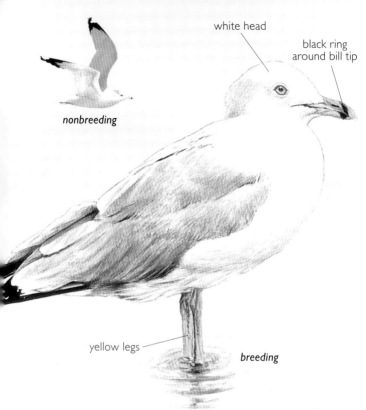

nonbreeding

white head

black ring
around bill tip

yellow legs

breeding

Nesting: along Lake Michigan's shores; colonial; in a shallow scrape on the ground lined with grass, debris and small sticks; brown-blotched, gray to olive eggs are 2⅜ x 1⅝ in; pair incubates 2–4 eggs for 23–28 days.

Did You Know?

This gull's population has exploded in recent years; a 2003 census of Indiana's breeding colonies yielded over 43,000 nests that contained eggs.

Look For

Ring-billed Gulls have a black ring around their bill and yellow legs, whereas similar-looking Herring Gulls have a red dot on their bill and pink legs.

Herring Gull

Larus argentatus

These gulls are as skilled at scrounging handouts on the beach as their smaller Ring-billed relatives, but Herring Gulls prefer wilderness areas over urban settings. They settle on lakes and large rivers where Ring-billed Gulls are not usually found. • When Herring Gulls arrive on their northern breeding grounds in spring, the landscape may still be covered in snow, but the gulls can stand on ice without freezing their feet. The arteries and veins in their legs run close together, so that blood flowing to the extremities warms the cooler blood traveling back to the core.

Other ID: yellow bill; light eyes; light gray mantle; white underparts. *Nonbreeding:* white head and nape are washed with brown.
Size: *L* 23–26 in; *W* 4 ft.
Voice: loud, buglelike *kleew-kleew*; also an alarmed *kak-kak-kak*.
Status: common on Lake Michigan in all seasons except summer; uncommon migrant elsewhere.
Habitat: large lakes, wetlands, rivers, landfills and urban areas.

Similar Birds

Ring-billed Gull
(p. 86)

Glaucous Gull

white-spotted, black wing tips

nonbreeding

white head

red spot on lower mandible

pink legs

breeding

Nesting: modest numbers nest in the large Ring-billed colonies along Lake Michigan's shores; singly or colonially; on an open beach or island; in a shallow scrape lined with vegetation and sticks; darkly blotched, olive to buff eggs are 2¾ x 1⅞ in; pair incubates 3 eggs for 31–32 days.

Did You Know?

Nestlings use the small, red spot on the gull's lower bill as a target; a hungry chick will peck at the spot, cueing the parent to regurgitate its meal.

Look For

Though Herring Gulls are skilled hunters, they are opportunistic and scavenge on human leftovers in fast-food parking lots and landfills.

Caspian Tern
Hydroprogne caspia

The North American population of Caspian Terns
has dramatically increased in the last half-century,
owing mainly to nesting habitat provided by
human-made dredge-spoil islands and dikes.
Adults ferociously defend breeding areas,
aggressively attacking and dive-bombing potential
predators. Nesting terns are extremely sensitive to
disturbance, and birders are advised to keep their
distance. • In size and habits, the Caspian Tern
bridges the gulf between the smaller terns and the
larger gulls.

Other ID: large, gull-like tern with black legs
and feet; moderately forked tail. *Nonbreeding:*
dusky crown and forehead. *In flight:* extensive
black visible on underwing.
Size: L 19–23 in; W 4–4¼ ft.
Voice: calls are low and harsh: *kaaar* or *kowk*.
Status: common, especially on Lake Michigan.
Habitat: beaches, mudflats, sandbars, lakes
and flooded agricultural fields.

Similar Birds

Forster's Tern
(p. 94)

Common Tern
(p. 92)

black cap includes
eyes and forehead

very pale upperparts

large, heavy, red
or red-orange bill

completely white
underparts

breeding

Nesting: colonial nester; on sand or gravel
beaches; pair constructs a shallow scrape,
sparsely lined with vegetation, rocks or other
debris; darkly spotted, pale buff or pinkish
eggs are 2½ x 1¾ in; pair incubates 2–3 eggs
for 20–22 days.

Did You Know?

In the Great Lakes region,
Caspian Terns are known
to live an average of 12
years, but the oldest wild
Caspian Tern lived more
than 26 years!

Look For

The Caspian Tern's distinctive, heavy, red-orange bill
and forked tail give away its
identity throughout its
worldwide range.

Common Tern
Sterna hirundo

Common Terns are sleek, agile birds. In spring
and fall, they patrol the shorelines of Lake
Michigan and are found locally on lakes and rivers
elsewhere in the state. Though Common Terns
have not nested in Indiana since 1936, they nest
elsewhere on the Great Lakes. To win a mate, the
male struts through the noisy
breeding colony with an offering
of fish in his mouth. If a female
accepts a suitor's gracious gift, they
pair up to nest.

Other ID: white underparts and rump; white tail
with gray outer edges. *Nonbreeding:* black nape; lacks
black cap. *In flight:* shallowly forked tail; long, pointed
wings; dark gray wedge on outer primaries.
Size: *L* 13–16 in; *W* 30 in.
Voice: high-pitched, drawn-out *keee-are;* most
commonly heard at colonies but also in
foraging flights.
Status: uncommon in spring and very common in fall on Lake Michigan; uncommon
elsewhere.
Habitat: large lakes, open wetlands, slow-
moving rivers, islands and beaches.

Similar Birds

Forster's Tern
(p. 94)

Caspian Tern
(p. 90)

black cap

black tip on
red bill

nonbreeding

white
underparts

red legs

white rump

breeding

Nesting: no longer nests in Indiana; nests in the northern U.S. and Canada; colonial; on an island; in a small scrape lined with pebbles, vegetation or shells; darkly blotched, creamy white eggs are 1⅝ x 1⅛ in; pair incubates 1–3 eggs for 20–24 days.

Did You Know?

Terns are effortless fliers and impressive long-distance migrants. Once, a Common Tern banded in Great Britain was recovered in Australia.

Look For

Terns hover over the water, then dive headfirst to capture small fish or aquatic invertebrates below the surface.

Forster's Tern

Sterna forsteri

The Forster's Tern so closely resembles the Common Tern that the two often seem indistinguishable. Only when these terns acquire their distinctive fall plumages do birders begin to note the Forster's presence. In Indiana, this is the most frequently encountered tern. • Forster's Tern has an exclusively North American breeding distribution, but it bears the name of German naturalist, Johann Reinhold Forster, who never visited this continent. Forster examined tern specimens sent from Hudson Bay, Canada, to England and was the first to recognize this bird as a distinct species.

Other ID: long, gray tail with white outer edges. *Breeding:* light gray mantle; white rump. *Nonbreeding:* black band through eyes; black bill. *In flight:* forked, gray tail; long, pointed wings; outer upperwings paler than back.
Size: L 14–16 in; W 31 in.
Voice: flight call is a nasal, short *keer keer;* also a grating *tzaap.*
Status: common migrant.
Habitat: freshwater lakes, rivers and marshes.

Similar Birds

Common Tern
(p. 92)

Caspian Tern
(p. 90)

black cap and nape

large, orange, black-tipped bill

pure white underparts

orange legs

breeding

Nesting: has not nested in Indiana since 1962; nests locally throughout North America; occasionally colonial; a platform of floating vegetation in freshwater or saltwater marshes; olive to buff, blotched eggs are 1⅝ x 1¼ in; pair incubates 2–3 eggs for 24 days.

Did You Know?

The bill color of the Forster's Tern changes from black in winter to orange with a black tip in summer.

Look For

Like most terns, the Forster's Tern catches fish in dramatic headfirst dives, but it also snatches flying insects in midair.

Rock Pigeon
Columba livia

Colorful and familiar Rock Pigeons have an unusual feature: they feed their young a substance similar to milk. These birds lack mammary glands, but they produce a nutritious liquid, called "pigeon milk," in their crops. To reach the thick, protein-rich fluid, a chick will insert its bill down the adult's throat. • This pigeon is likely a descendant of a Eurasian bird that was first domesticated about 4500 BCE. European settlers introduced the Rock Pigeon to North America in the 17th century.

Other ID: usually has white rump and orange feet. *In flight:* holds wings in a deep "V" while gliding.
Size: L 12–13 in; W 28 in (male is usually larger).
Voice: soft, cooing *coorrr-coorrr-coorrr.*
Status: common in urban areas.
Habitat: urban areas, railroad yards and agricultural areas; high cliffs often provide more natural habitat.

Similar Birds

Eurasian Collared-Dove
(p. 98)

Mourning Dove
(p. 100)

color is highly variable
(iridescent blue-gray,
red, white or tan)

white
cere

Nesting: in a barn or on a cliff, bridge or
tower; in a flimsy nest of sticks, grass and other
vegetation; glossy white eggs are 1½ x 1⅛ in;
pair incubates 2 eggs for 16–19 days; may raise
broods year-round.

Did You Know?

Both Julius Caesar and
Napoleon Bonaparte used
Rock Pigeons as message
couriers.

Look For

No other "wild" bird varies
as much in coloration, a
result of semidomestication
and extensive inbreeding
over time.

Eurasian Collared-Dove

Streptopelia decaocto

The colonization of North America by the Eurasian Collared-Dove has been astonishing. From perhaps 50 doves released in the Bahamas in 1974, the birds reached the southeastern Florida peninsula probably in the late 1970s. However, they were misidentified as a similar species for years and not formally "discovered" there until 1986. Eurasian Collared-Doves have now colonized much of the continent, and they were first detected in Indiana during the summer of 1999.

Other ID: a large, chunky dove; square tail with white outertail feathers.
Size: *L* 12–13 in; *W* 18–20 in.
Voice: a low *coo-coo, COOK,* repeated incessantly throughout the day.
Status: locally uncommon, but numbers are increasing dramatically.
Habitat: primarily associated with humans; urban and suburban areas, especially along the coasts; also dairy farms.

Similar Birds

Mourning Dove
(p. 100)

Rock Pigeon
(p. 96)

black hind-collar is outlined in white

pale gray overall (paler than Mourning Dove)

dark wing tips

Nesting: in a tree; female builds a platform of twigs and sticks; white eggs are 1¼ x ⅞ in; pair incubates 2 eggs for about 14 days; may raise 3 or more broods in a season.

Did You Know?

Native to India and Southeast Asia, these doves have greatly expanded their range to include Europe, Africa and other parts of Asia.

Look For

Eurasian Collared-Doves feed on grain and seeds, and are frequent visitors to bird feeders.

Mourning Dove
Zenaida macroura

The Mourning Dove's soft cooing, which filters
through broken woodlands and suburban parks,
is often confused with the sound of a hooting owl.
Beginning birders who track down the source of
the calls are often surprised to find the stream-
lined silhouette of a perched dove. • This popular
game animal is common throughout Indiana and
is one of the most abundant native birds in North
America. Its numbers and range have increased
since human development has created more open
habitats and food sources, such as waste grain and
bird feeders.

Other ID: buffy, gray-brown plumage; small
head; dark bill; sleek body; dull red legs.
Size: *L* 11–13 in; *W* 18 in.
Voice: mournful, soft, slow *oh-woe-woe-woe*.
Status: common.
Habitat: open and riparian woodlands, forest
edges, agricultural and suburban areas, open
parks.

Similar Birds

Eurasian Collared-Dove
(p. 98)

Rock Pigeon
(p. 96)

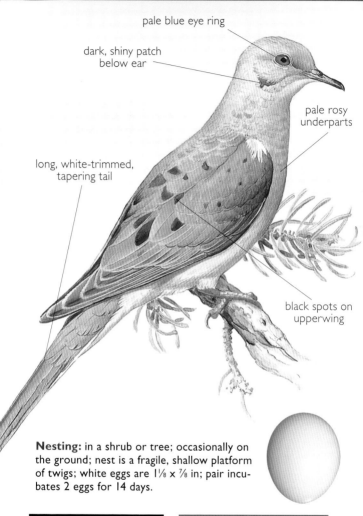

pale blue eye ring

dark, shiny patch
below ear

pale rosy
underparts

long, white-trimmed,
tapering tail

black spots on
upperwing

Nesting: in a shrub or tree; occasionally on the ground; nest is a fragile, shallow platform of twigs; white eggs are 1⅛ x ⅞ in; pair incubates 2 eggs for 14 days.

Did You Know?

The Mourning Dove raises up to six broods each year—more than any other native bird.

Look For

When the Mourning Dove bursts into flight, its wings clap above and below its body. It also often creates a whistling sound as it flies at high speed.

Yellow-billed Cuckoo
Coccyzus americanus

Large tracts of hardwood forest with plenty of
clearings, such as the Hoosier National Forest,
provide valuable habitat for the Yellow-billed
Cuckoo, a bird that is declining over much of its
range and has already disappeared from some
states. The cuckoo's habitat is also steadily disap-
pearing as waterways are altered or dammed.
• The cuckoo silently negotiates its tangled home
within impenetrable, deciduous undergrowth,
relying on obscurity for survival. Then, for a short
period during nesting, the male cuckoo tempts
fate by issuing a barrage of loud, rhythmic courtship calls.

Other ID: olive brown upperparts; white
underparts. *In flight:* rufous in outer wing.
Size: *L* 11–13 in; *W* 18 in.
Voice: long series of deep, hollow *kuks*, slow-
ing near the end: *kuk-kuk-kuk-kuk kuk kop kow
kowlp kowlp*.
Status: fairly common, but more commonly
heard than seen.
Habitat: semi-open deciduous habitats; dense
tangles and thickets at the edges of orchards,
urban parks, agricultural fields and roadways;
sometimes woodlots.

Similar Birds

Black-billed Cuckoo

Mourning Dove
(p. 100)

Eurasian Collared-Dove
(p. 98)

yellowish eye ring

rufous tinge on primaries

mainly yellow, slightly down-curved bill with black upper ridge

long tail with large, white spots on underside

Nesting: on a low, horizontal branch in a deciduous shrub or small tree, flimsy platform nest of twigs is lined with grass; pale bluish green eggs are 1¼ x ⅞ in; pair incubates 3–4 eggs for 9–11 days.

Did You Know?

The Yellow-billed Cuckoo, or "Rain Crow," has a propensity for calling on dark, cloudy days and a reputation for predicting rainstorms.

Look For

Yellow-billed Cuckoos produce more young when outbreaks of cicadas or tent caterpillars provide an abundant food supply.

Eastern Screech-Owl
Megascops asio

red morph

The diminutive Eastern Screech-Owl is a year-round resident of low-elevation, deciduous woodlands, but its presence is rarely detected—most screech-owls sleep away the daylight hours. The noise of a mobbing horde of chickadees or a squawking gang of Blue Jays can alert you to an owl's presence during the day. Smaller birds often mob a screech-owl after losing a family member during the night. • Eastern Screech-Owls show both red and gray color morphs. In Indiana, both morphs are common, with the grays having a slight edge. One hundred years ago, though, reds were the more common morph. Very rarely, an intermediate brown morph occurs.

Other ID: small; reddish or grayish overall; yellow eyes; pale grayish bill.
Size: L 8–9 in; W 20–22 in.
Voice: horselike "whinny" that rises and falls.
Status: common, but numbers have declined over the last 50 years.
Habitat: mature deciduous forests, open deciduous and riparian woodlands, orchards and shade trees with natural cavities.

Similar Birds

Northern Saw-whet Owl

Long-eared Owl

short
"ear" tufts

dark breast
streaking

gray morph

Nesting: in an unlined natural cavity or artificial nest box; white eggs are 1½ x 1¼ in; female incubates 4–5 eggs for about 26 days; male brings food to the female during incubation.

Did You Know?

The Eastern Screech-Owl has one of the most varied diets of any owl. It will capture small animals, earthworms, insects and even fish.

Look For

Eastern Screech-Owls respond readily to whistled imitations of their calls, and sometimes several owls will appear to investigate the fraudulent perpetrator.

Great Horned Owl
Bubo virginianus

This highly adaptable and superbly camouflaged hunter has sharp hearing and powerful vision that allow it to hunt at night as well as by day. It will swoop down from a perch onto almost any small creature that moves. • An owl has specially designed feathers on its wings to reduce noise. The leading edge of the flight feathers is fringed rather than smooth, which interrupts airflow over the wing and allows the owl to fly noiselessly. • Great Horned Owls begin their courtship as early as January, and by February and March, the females are already incubating their eggs.

Other ID: overall plumage varies from light gray to dark brown; heavily mottled, gray, brown and black upperparts; yellow eyes; white chin.
Size: *L* 18–25 in; *W* 3–5 ft.
Voice: breeding call is 4–6 deep hoots: *hoo-hoo-hoooo hoo-hoo* or *Who's awake? Me too;* female gives higher-pitched hoots.
Status: common and widespread.
Habitat: fragmented forests, fields, riparian woodlands, suburban parks and wooded edges of landfills.

Similar Birds

Long-eared Owl

Look For

Owls regurgitate pellets that contain the indigestible parts of their prey. You can find these dry, clean pellets under frequently used perches.

tall, widely spaced "ear" tufts form a triangle with bill

rusty orange facial disc is outlined in black

fine, horizontal barring on breast

Nesting: in another bird's abandoned stick nest or in a tree cavity; adds little or no nest material; dull whitish eggs are 2¼ x 1⅞ in; mostly the female incubates 2–3 eggs for 28–35 days.

Did You Know?

A Great Horned Owl's eyes are unable to move in their sockets the way a human's eyes can. However, this owl is able to look in any direction it wants—its flexible neck can turn 180 degrees to the left or the right. In contrast to its acute vision, the Great Horned Owl has a poor sense of smell, which may explain why it is the only consistent predator of skunks.

Barred Owl
Strix varia

The adaptable Barred Owl is found in many woodland habitats throughout Indiana, especially those near water. It uses large tracts of mature forest, ranging from swampy bottomlands to higher, mixed forests. • Each spring, the escalating laughs, hoots and gargling howls of Barred Owls reinforce their pair bonds. These owls tend to be most vocal during late evening and early morning when the moon is full, the air is calm and the sky is clear.

Other ID: mottled, dark gray-brown plumage.
Size: *L* 17–24 in; *W* 3½–4 ft.
Voice: loud, hooting, rhythmic, laughing call is heard mostly in spring: *Who cooks for you? Who cooks for you all?*
Status: common along wooded streams and wet bottomlands.
Habitat: mature coniferous and mixed wood forests, especially in dense stands near swamps, streams and lakes.

Similar Birds

Short-eared Owl

Look For

Dark eyes make the Barred Owl unique—most familiar large owls in North America have yellow eyes.

no "ear" tufts

dark eyes

pale bill

horizontal barring around neck and upper breast

vertical streaking on belly

Nesting: in a natural tree cavity, broken tree-top or abandoned stick nest; adds very little material to the nest; white eggs are 2 x 1⅝ in; female incubates 2–3 eggs for 28–33 days.

Did You Know?

In darkness, the Barred Owl's eyesight may be 100 times keener than that of humans. This owl is also able to locate and follow prey using sound alone. It is an opportunistic predator, preying on all kinds of other animals, including mammals, amphibians, reptiles, other birds and some invertebrates.

Common Nighthawk
Chordeiles minor

The Common Nighthawk makes an unforgettable booming sound as it flies high overhead. In an energetic courting display, the male dives, then swerves skyward, making a hollow *vroom* sound with his wings. • Like other members of the nightjar family, the Common Nighthawk is well adapted for catching insects in midair: its large, gaping mouth is surrounded by feather shafts that funnel insects into its bill. A nighthawk can eat over 2600 insects in one day, including mosquitoes, blackflies and flying ants. • Look for nighthawks foraging for insects at nighttime baseball games.

Other ID: *Female:* buff throat. *In flight:* shallowly forked, barred tail; erratic flight.
Size: *L* 8–10 in; *W* 23–26 in.
Voice: frequently repeated, nasal *peent peent*; wings make a deep, hollow *vroom* during a courtship dive.
Status: species of special concern as a breeder.
Habitat: *Breeding:* forest openings, bogs, rocky outcroppings and gravel rooftops.
In migration: often near water; any area with large numbers of flying insects.

Similar Birds

Chuck-will's-widow   Whip-poor-will
                                  (p. 112)

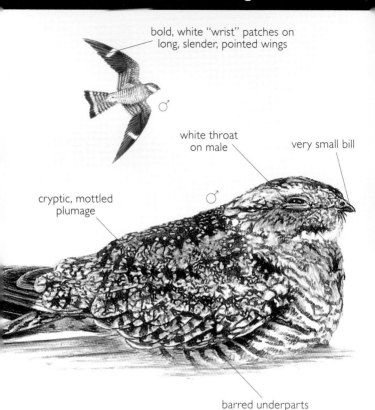

bold, white "wrist" patches on long, slender, pointed wings

white throat on male

very small bill

cryptic, mottled plumage

barred underparts

Nesting: on bare ground; no nest is built; heavily marked, creamy white to buff eggs are 1⅛ x ⅞ in; female incubates 2 eggs for about 19 days; both adults feed the young.

Did You Know?

Nighthawk population numbers have declined in Indiana over the past 50 years.

Look For

Impressive fall flights, sometimes consisting of hundreds of southbound birds, occur in late August and early September.

Whip-poor-will

Caprimulgus vociferus

These magical, elusive birds blend seamlessly into lichen-covered bark or the forest floor. On spring evenings, their airy, soothing *whip-poor-will* calls float through the open woodlands, signaling their availability to prospective mates. • Ground-nesting Whip-poor-wills time their egg-laying to the lunar cycle so that hatchlings can be fed more efficiently during the light of the full moon. For the first 20 days after hatching, until the young are able to fly, the parents feed them regurgitated insects.

Other ID: mottled brown-gray overall with black flecking; large eyes; dark throat; relatively long, rounded tail. *Male:* white outer tail feathers. *Female:* buff "necklace"; buffy outer tail feathers.
Size: L 9–10 in; W 16–20 in.
Voice: whistled *whip-poor-will*, with emphasis on the *will*.
Status: species of special concern with declining numbers.
Habitat: open deciduous and pine woodlands; often along forest edges.

Similar Birds

Chuck-will's-widow

Common Nighthawk
(p. 110)

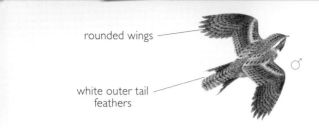

rounded wings

white outer tail
feathers

♂

dark stripe runs down
center of crown

♂

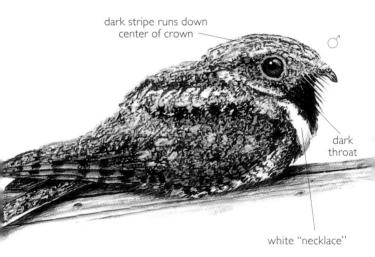

dark
throat

white "necklace"

Nesting: on the ground in leaf or pine needle
litter; no nest is built; whitish eggs with brown
blotches are 1¼ x ⅞ in; female incubates 2 eggs
for 19–20 days; both adults raise the young.

Did You Know?

Within days of hatching,
young Whip-poor-wills
can scurry away from
their nest in search of
protective cover if
disturbed.

Look For

Good Indiana populations
remain at Willow Slough Fish
and Wildlife Area and at Big
Oaks National Wildlife
Refuge.

Ruby-throated Hummingbird

Archilochus colubris

Ruby-throated Hummingbirds feed on sweet, energy-rich flower nectar and pollinate flowers in the process. You can attract hummingbirds to your backyard with a red nectar feeder filled with a sugarwater solution (red food coloring is both unnecessary and harmful to the birds) or with native, nectar-producing flowers such as honeysuckle or bee balm. • Each year, Ruby-throated Hummingbirds migrate across the Gulf of Mexico—a nonstop, 500-mile journey. They may lose up to a third of their body weight while making this flight.

Other ID: thin, needlelike bill; pale underparts.
Size: *L* 3½–4 in; *W* 4–4½ in.
Voice: a loud *chick* and other high squeaks; soft buzzing of the wings while in flight.
Status: common, especially in late August and early September.
Habitat: open, mixed woodlands, wetlands, orchards, tree-lined meadows, flower gardens and backyards with trees and feeders.

Look For

A female Ruby-throated Hummingbird has a greenish back and white throat. Nonbreeding males have dark brown to black throats.

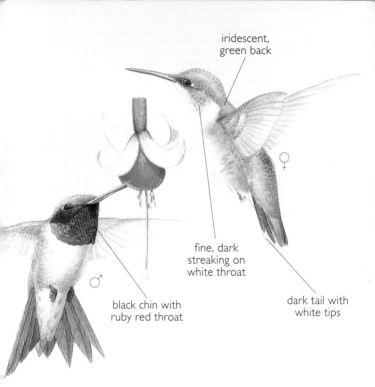

iridescent, green back

♀

fine, dark streaking on white throat

♂

black chin with ruby red throat

dark tail with white tips

Nesting: on a horizontal tree limb; tiny, deep cup nest of plant down and fibers is held together with spider silk; lichens and leaves are pasted on the exterior walls; white eggs are ½ x ⅜ in; female incubates 2 eggs for 13–16 days.

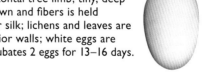

Did You Know?

Weighing about as much as a nickel, a hummingbird can briefly reach speeds of up to 60 miles per hour. In straight-ahead flight, hummingbirds beat their wings up to 80 times per second, and their hearts can beat up to 1200 times per minute! They are among the few birds that can fly vertically and in reverse.

Belted Kingfisher
Ceryle alcyon

Perched on a bare branch over a productive pool, the Belted Kingfisher utters a scratchy, rattling call. Then, with little regard for its scruffy hair-do, the "king of the fishers" plunges headfirst into the water and snags a fish or a frog. Back on land, the kingfisher flips its prey into the air and swallows it headfirst. Similar to owls, kingfishers regurgitate the indigestible portion of their food as pellets, which can be found beneath favorite perches.

Other ID: bluish upperparts; small, white patch near eye; straight bill; short legs; white underwings.
Size: *L* 11–14 in; *W* 20–21 in.
Voice: fast, repetitive, cackling rattle, like a teacup shaking on a saucer.
Status: uncommon to fairly common.
Habitat: rivers, large streams, lakes, marshes and beaver ponds, especially near exposed soil banks, gravel pits or bluffs.

Similar Birds

Blue Jay
(p. 138)

Look For

The Belted Kingfisher often flies very close to the water, so close, in fact, that its wing tips may skim the surface.

shaggy crest

white collar

♀

♂

blue-gray
breast band

rust-colored belt
on female may be
incomplete

Nesting: in a cavity at the end of an earth
burrow; glossy white eggs are 1⅜ x 1 in; pair
incubates 6–7 eggs for 22–24 days.

Did You Know?

Kingfisher pairs nest on sandy banks, taking turns digging
a tunnel with their sturdy bills and claws. Nest burrows may
measure up to 6 feet long and are often found near water.
Once the young are at least five days old, the parents return
to the nest regularly with small fingerling fish, which the nestlings eat whole.

Red-headed Woodpecker
Melanerpes erythrocephalus

This bird of the East lives mostly in open deciduous woodlands, urban parks and oak savannahs.
Red-heads were once common throughout their
range, but their numbers have declined dramatically over the past century. Since the introduction
of the European Starling, these woodpeckers have
been largely outcompeted for nesting cavities.
• These birds are frequent traffic fatalities, often
struck by vehicles when they dart from their
perches and over roadways to catch flying insects.

Other ID: white underparts; black tail.
Juvenile: brown back, wings and tail; slight brown
streaking on white underparts.
Size: *L* 9–9½ in; *W* 17 in.
Voice: loud series of *kweer* or *kwrring* notes;
occasionally a chattering *kerr-r-ruck*; also drums
softly in short bursts.
Status: common but local.
Habitat: open deciduous woodlands (especially oak woodlands), urban parks, river edges
and roadsides with groves of scattered trees.

Similar Birds

Red-bellied Woodpecker
(p. 120)

Yellow-bellied
Sapsucker

bright red head

black back
and wings

large, white patch

brown head

white
lower
back

juvenile

Nesting: male excavates a nest cavity in a
dead tree or limb; white eggs are 1 x ¾ in; pair
incubates 4–5 eggs for 12–13 days; both adults
feed the young.

Did You Know?

The Red-headed
Woodpecker is one of
only four woodpecker
species that regularly
cache food.

Look For

The forested bottomlands,
swamps and semi-open habitats of Indiana are favorite
haunts of this charismatic
bird.

Red-bellied Woodpecker
Melanerpes carolinus

The familiar Red-bellied Woodpecker is no stranger to suburban backyards and sometimes nests in birdhouses. This widespread bird is found year-round in woodlands throughout the eastern states, but numbers fluctuate depending on habitat availability and weather conditions. • Unlike most woodpeckers, Red-bellies consume large amounts of plant material, seldom excavating wood for insects. • When occupying an area together with Red-headed Woodpeckers, Red-bellies will nest in the trunk, below the foliage, and the Red-heads will nest in dead branches among the foliage.

Other ID: reddish tinge on lower belly.
Juvenile: dark gray crown; streaked breast.
Size: *L* 9–10½ in; *W* 16 in.
Voice: call is a soft, rolling *churr*; drums in second-long bursts.
Status: common.
Habitat: mature deciduous woodlands; sometimes in wooded residential areas; occasionally visits feeding stations.

Similar Birds

Northern Flicker
(p. 124)

Red-headed Woodpecker
(p. 118)

black and white barring on back

red nape extends to forehead

♂

red nape

♀

white patches on rump are speckled with black

Nesting: nests in woodlands or residential areas; in a cavity excavated mainly by the male; white eggs are 1 x ¾ in; pair incubates 4–5 eggs for 12–14 days; both adults raise the young.

Did You Know?

Studies of banded Red-bellied Woodpeckers have shown that these birds have a lifespan in the wild of more than 20 years.

Look For

This bird's namesake, its red belly, is only a small reddish area that is difficult to see in the field.

Downy Woodpecker
Picoides pubescens

A pair of Downy Woodpeckers at your backyard bird feeder will brighten a frosty winter day. These approachable little birds are more tolerant of human activity than most other species, and they visit feeders more often than the larger, more aggressive Hairy Woodpeckers *(P. villosus)*. • Like other woodpeckers, the Downy has evolved special features to help cushion the shock of repeated hammering, including a strong bill and neck muscles, a flexible, reinforced skull and a brain that is tightly packed in its protective cranium.

Other ID: black eye line and crown; white patch on back; white belly. *Male:* small, red patch on back of head. *Female:* no red patch.
Size: L 6–7 in; W 12 in.
Voice: long, unbroken trill; calls are a sharp *pik* or *ki-ki-ki* or whiny *queek queek*.
Status: common and widespread.
Habitat: any wooded environment, especially deciduous and mixed forests and areas with tall, deciduous shrubs.

Similar Birds

Hairy Woodpecker

Yellow-bellied
Sapsucker

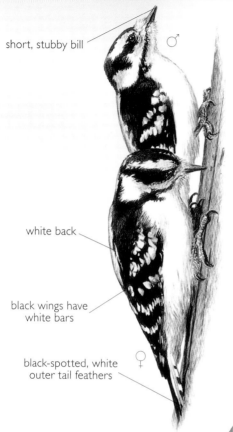

short, stubby bill

♂

white back

black wings have
white bars

black-spotted, white
outer tail feathers

♀

Nesting: pair excavates a cavity in a dying
or decaying trunk and lines it with wood
chips; white eggs are ¾ x ⅝ in; pair
incubates 4–5 eggs for 11–13 days.

Did You Know?

Woodpeckers have feath-
ered nostrils, which filter
out the sawdust produced
by hammering.

Look For

Both the Downy Woodpecker
and Hairy Woodpecker have
white outer tail feathers, but
the Downy's have dark spots
while the Hairy's are pure
white.

Northern Flicker
Colaptes auratus

Instead of boring holes in trees, the Northern Flicker scours the ground in search of invertebrates, particularly ants. With robinlike hops, it investigates anthills, grassy meadows and forest clearings. • Flickers often bathe in dusty depressions. The dust particles absorb oils and bacteria that can harm the birds' feathers. To clean themselves even more thoroughly, flickers squash ants and preen themselves with the remains. Ants contain formic acid, which kills small parasites on the birds' skin and feathers.

Other ID: long bill; brownish to buff face; gray crown; white rump. *Male:* black "mustache" stripe. *Female:* no "mustache."
Size: L 12–13 in; W 20 in.
Voice: loud, "laughing," rapid *kick-kick-kick-kick-kick-kick; woika-woika-woika* issued during courtship.
Status: common.
Habitat: *Breeding:* open woodlands and forest edges; fields, meadows, beaver ponds and other wetlands. *In migration* and *winter:* urban gardens.

Similar Birds

Red-bellied
Woodpecker
(p. 120)

Yellow-bellied
Sapsucker

red nape crescent

brown, barred back and wings ♂

black "bib"

"Yellow-shafted Flicker"

yellow underwings and undertail

♀

black-spotted, buff to whitish underparts

Nesting: pair excavates a cavity in a dying or decaying trunk and lines it with wood chips; may also use a nest box; white eggs are 1⅛ x ⅞ in; pair incubates 5–8 eggs for 11–16 days.

Did You Know?

The very long tongue of a woodpecker wraps around twin structures in the skull and is stored like a measuring tape in its case.

Look For

In April, large numbers of flickers can be observed migrating along the Lake Michigan shoreline in the Indiana dunes. Daily counts can exceed 500 birds.

Pileated Woodpecker
Dryocopus pileatus

The Pileated Woodpecker, with its flaming red crest, chisel-like bill and commanding size, requires 100 acres of mature forest as a home territory. In our region, the patchwork of woodlots and small towns limits the availability of continuous habitat, requiring this woodpecker to show itself more. • A pair of woodpeckers will spend up to six weeks excavating a large nest cavity in a dead or decaying tree. Wood Ducks, kestrels, owls and even flying squirrels frequently nest in abandoned Pileated Woodpecker cavities.

Other ID: crow-sized bird; predominantly black; yellow eyes; white chin. *Male:* red "mustache." *Female:* no red "mustache"; gray-brown forehead.
Size: L 16–17 in; W 28–29 in.
Voice: loud, fast, rolling *woika-woika-woika-woika* long series of *kuk* notes; loud, resonant drumming.
Status: common in dense woodlands.
Habitat: extensive tracts of mature forests; also riparian woodlands or woodlots in suburban and agricultural areas.

Look For

In Indiana, Pileated Woodpeckers are slowly expanding their range northward. Foraging Pileated Woodpeckers leave large, rectangular cavities up to 12 inches long near the base of trees.

flaming red crest extends farther on male

stout, dark bill

♂

white stripe runs from bill to shoulder

♀

white wing linings

Nesting: pair excavates a cavity in a dying or decaying trunk and lines it with wood chips; white eggs are 1¼ x 1 in; pair incubates 4 eggs for 15–18 days.

Did You Know?

Even outside of the breeding season, Pileated Woodpeckers will spend the night in tree cavities. Adult woodpeckers may have multiple roost sites to choose from on their territories.

Eastern Wood-Pewee
Contopus virens

Our most common and widespread woodland fly-catcher, the Eastern Wood-Pewee, breeds in every county in Indiana. The male is readily detected by his plaintive, whistled *pee-ah-wee pee-oh* song, which is repeated all day long throughout summer. Some of the keenest suitors will even sing their charms late into the evening. • Like most flycatchers, the Eastern Wood-Pewee darts from its perch to snatch flying insects in midair, then returns to the same perch to enjoy its prize. This small flycatcher will even capture insects as large as swallowtail butterflies and dragonflies.

Other ID: slender body; olive gray to olive brown upperparts; whitish throat; gray breast and sides; whitish or pale yellow belly, flanks and undertail coverts.
Size: *L* 6–6½ in; *W* 10 in.
Voice: *Male:* song is a clear, slow, plaintive *pee-ah-wee*, with the second note lower, followed by a down-slurred *pee-oh*, with or without intermittent pauses; also a *chip* call.
Status: common in summer and migration.
Habitat: open mixed and deciduous woodlands with a sparse understory, especially woodland openings and edges; rarely in open coniferous woodlands.

Similar Birds

Olive-sided Flycatcher

Willow Flycatcher

Eastern Phoebe
(p. 130)

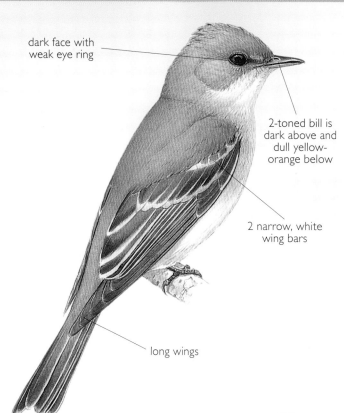

dark face with
weak eye ring

2-toned bill is
dark above and
dull yellow-
orange below

2 narrow, white
wing bars

long wings

Nesting: on the fork of a horizontal deciduous branch, well away from the trunk; open cup of plants and lichen is bound with spider silk; whitish, darkly blotched eggs are 1 x ⁹⁄₁₆ in; female incubates 3 eggs for 12–13 days.

Did You Know?

Camouflage or a poisonous or distasteful nature are defense mechanisms used by insects to avert predators, such as wood-pewees.

Look For

This bird tolerates human activity and may be found in open woodlands, including urban parks and gardens.

Eastern Phoebe
Sayornis phoebe

Whether you are poking around a barnyard, a campground picnic shelter or your backyard shed, there is a very good chance that you will stumble upon an Eastern Phoebe family and its marvelous mud nest. The Eastern Phoebe's nest-building and territorial defense is normally well underway by the time most other songbirds arrive in Indiana in mid-May. Once limited to nesting on natural cliffs and fallen riparian trees, this adaptive flycatcher has found success nesting in culverts and under bridges and eaves, especially when water is nearby.

Other ID: gray-brown upperparts; belly may be washed with yellow in fall; no eye ring; weak wing bars; dark legs.
Size: L 6½–7 in; W 10½ in.
Voice: song is a hearty, snappy *fee-bee*, delivered frequently; call is a sharp *chip*.
Status: common.
Habitat: open deciduous woodlands, forest edges and clearings; usually near water.

Similar Birds

Eastern Wood-Pewee
(p. 128)

Least Flycatcher

Willow Flycatcher

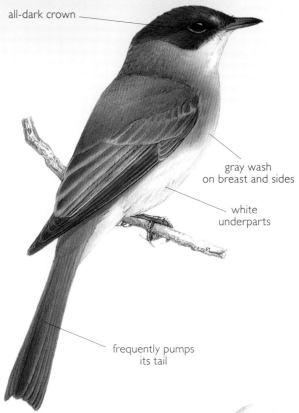

all-dark crown

gray wash
on breast and sides

white
underparts

frequently pumps
its tail

Nesting: under the ledge of a building, picnic shelter, culvert, bridge, cliff or well; cup-shaped mud nest is lined with soft material; white, red-spotted eggs are ¾ x 9/16 in; female incubates 4–5 eggs for about 16 days.

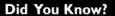

Did You Know?

Eastern Phoebes often reuse their nest sites for many years. Females that save energy by reusing their nests are often able to lay more eggs.

Look For

Some other birds pump their tails while perched, but few species can match the zest and frequency of the Eastern Phoebe's tail pumping.

Great Crested Flycatcher

Myiarchus crinitus

Loud, raucous calls give away the presence of the brightly colored Great Crested Flycatcher. This large flycatcher often inhabits forest edges, and it nests in woodlands throughout Indiana. Unlike other eastern flycatchers, the Great Crested Flycatcher prefers to nest in a tree cavity or abandoned woodpecker hole, or sometimes uses a nest box intended for a bluebird. Instead of cutting down large, dead trees, consider leaving a few standing. Many animals depend on tree cavities for shelter and nesting.

Other ID: yellow underparts; dark olive brown upperparts; heavy, black bill.
Size: *L* 8–9 in; *W* 13 in.
Voice: loud, whistled *wheep!* and a rolling *prrrrreet!*
Status: common.
Habitat: deciduous and mixed woodlands and forests, usually near openings or edges.

Similar Birds

Western Kingbird

Look For

Follow the loud *wheep!* calls and watch for a show of bright yellow and rufous feathers to find this flycatcher.

peaked head with small crest

gray throat and upper breast

bright yellow belly and undertail coverts

reddish brown tail

Nesting: in a tree cavity or nest box; nest is lined with soft material; may hang a shed snakeskin from the entrance hole; heavily marked, creamy white to pale buff eggs are ⅞ x ⅝ in; female incubates 5 eggs for 13–15 days.

Did You Know?

The Great Crested Flycatcher will sometimes decorate its nest entrance with a shed snakeskin or substitute translucent plastic wrap. The purpose of this practice is not fully understood, though it might make any potential predators think twice.

Eastern Kingbird
Tyrannus tyrannus

Sometimes referred to as the "Jekyll and Hyde" bird, the Eastern Kingbird is a gregarious fruit eater while wintering in South America, and an antisocial, aggressive insect eater while nesting in North America. • The Eastern Kingbird fearlessly attacks crows, hawks and even humans that pass through its territory, pursuing and pecking at them until the threat has passed. No one familiar with the Eastern Kingbird's pugnacious behavior will refute its scientific name, *Tyrannus tyrannus*, but this bird reveals a gentler side of its character in its quivering, butterfly-like courtship flight.

Other ID: black bill; no eye ring; white underparts; grayish breast; black legs.
Size: L 8½–9 in; W 15 in.
Voice: call is a quick, loud, chattering *kit-kit-kitter-kitter;* also a buzzy *dzee-dzee-dzee.*
Status: common and widespread.
Habitat: fields with scattered shrubs, trees or hedgerows; forest fringes, clearings, shrubby roadsides, towns and farmyards.

Similar Birds

Olive-sided Flycatcher

Look For

On a drive in the country you will likely spot at least one of these common and widespread birds sitting on a fence or utility wire.

small head crest

thin, orange-red crown
(very rarely seen)

dark gray to black
upperparts

white-tipped tail

Nesting: on a horizontal limb, stump or
upturned tree root; cup nest is made of weeds,
twigs and grass; darkly blotched, white to pinkish white eggs are 1 x ¾ in; female incubates
3–4 eggs for 14–18 days.

Did You Know?

These birds are excellent fliers—they need to be in order to
catch enough insects in a day to feed themselves and their
young. In fact, flycatchers lay relatively small clutches, in part
because insects are so much work to obtain for their
offspring.

Red-eyed Vireo
Vireo olivaceus

Capable of delivering about 40 phrases per minute, the male Red-eyed Vireo can out-sing any one of his courting neighbors. One tenacious male set a record by singing 21,000 phrases in one day! Although you may still hear the Red-eyed Vireo singing five or six hours after other songbirds have ceased for the day, this bird is not easy to spot. Its olive green plumage usually keeps it concealed among the foliage of deciduous trees. Its unique red eyes, unusual among songbirds, are even trickier to spot without a good pair of binoculars.

Other ID: black-bordered, olive cheek; olive green upperparts; white to pale gray underparts.
Size: L 6 in; W 10 in.
Voice: call is a short, scolding *rreeah*.
Male: song is a series of quick, continuous, variable phrases with pauses in between: *look-up, way-up, tree-top, see-me, here-I-am!*
Status: common in woodlands.
Habitat: deciduous or mixed woodlands with a shrubby understory.

Similar Birds

Philadelphia Vireo   Warbling Vireo   Tennessee Warbler

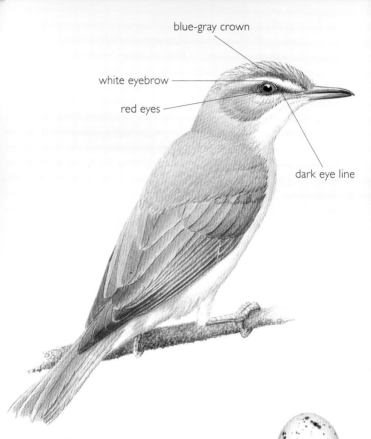

blue-gray crown

white eyebrow

red eyes

dark eye line

Nesting: in a tree or shrub; hanging cup nest is made of grass, roots, spider silk and cocoons; darkly spotted, white eggs are ¾ x ½ in; female incubates 4 eggs for 11–14 days.

Did You Know?

More than 100 singing Red-eyed Vireos have been detected in a single day, rendering this species among Indiana's most common songbirds.

Look For

The Red-eyed Vireo perches with a hunched stance and hops with its body turned diagonally to its direction of travel.

Blue Jay

Cyanocitta cristata

In Indiana, the Blue Jay is the only member of the corvid family dressed in blue. White-flecked wing feathers and sharply defined facial features make this bird easy to recognize. • Jays can be quite aggressive when competing for sunflower seeds and peanuts at backyard feeding stations and rarely hesitate to drive away smaller birds, squirrels or threatening cats. Even the Great Horned Owl is not too formidable a predator for a group of these brave, boisterous birds to harass.

Other ID: blue upperparts; white underparts; black bill.
Size: *L* 11–12 in; *W* 16 in.
Voice: noisy, screaming *jay-jay-jay;* nasal *queedle queedle queedle-queedle* sounds like a muted trumpet; often imitates various sounds, including calls of other birds.
Status: common and widespread.
Habitat: mixed deciduous forests, agricultural areas, scrubby fields and townsites.

Similar Birds

Belted Kingfisher
(p. 116)

Look For

Large spring migrations occur along the shores of Lake Michigan in May. Hundreds of Blue Jays have been counted flying eastward in a single day.

blue crest

white flecking and
dark bars on wings

black "necklace"

dark bars and
white corners on
blue tail

Nesting: in a tree or tall shrub; pair builds
a bulky stick nest; greenish, buff or pale eggs,
spotted with gray and brown, are 1⅛ x ¾ in;
pair incubates 4–5 eggs for 16–18 days.

Did You Know?

Blue Jays store food from feeders in trees and other places
for later use. In preparation for winter food shortages, a single bird may cache 3000 to 5000 nuts in a single fall season!
While transporting food to a cache site, a Blue Jay may fill its
distended throat, as well as its mouth and bill in order to
transport as much as possible in a single trip.

American Crow
Corvus brachyrhynchos

The noise that most often emanates from this treetop squawker seems unrepresentative of its intelligence. However, this wary, clever bird is also an impressive mimic, able to whine like a dog and laugh or cry like a human. • American Crows have flourished in spite of considerable efforts, over many generations, to reduce their numbers. As ecological generalists, crows can survive in a wide variety of habitats and conditions. In January, when crows in Indiana are searching snow-covered fields for mice or carrion, crows in more southerly locales are busy capturing frogs and lizards in thriving wetlands.

Other ID: glossy, black plumage; black bill and legs.
Size: L 17–21 in; W 3 ft.
Voice: distinctive, far-carrying, repetitive *caw-caw-caw*.
Status: common.
Habitat: urban areas, agricultural fields and other open areas with scattered woodlands.

Similar Birds

Common Grackle
(p. 216)

Look For

Crows will drop nuts or clams onto a hard surface to crack the shells, one of the few examples of birds using objects to manipulate food.

short, square-shaped tail

slim, sleek head
and throat

Nesting: in a tree or on a utility pole; large stick-and-branch nest is lined with fur and soft plant materials; darkly blotched, gray-green to blue-green eggs are 1⅝ x 1⅛ in; female incubates 4–6 eggs for about 18 days.

Did You Know?

Highly social corvids are among the most clever birds. They have superb memories and are able to learn, make simple tools and problem solve. They even exhibit some behaviors that can only be construed as play: young will play-fight or have "tugs of war" with twigs or other objects.

Horned Lark
Eremophila alpestris

Performing an impressive, high-speed, plummeting courtship dive would blow back anybody's hair, or in the case of the Horned Lark, its two unique black "horns." From as high up as 800 feet, the male performs his dramatic courtship display just after issuing his sweet, tinkling song, one of the first songs you'll hear in spring. • Horned Larks are often abundant at roadsides, searching for seeds, but an approaching vehicle usually sends them flying into an adjacent field.

Other ID: *Male:* light yellow to white face; pale throat; dull brown upperparts. *Female:* duller plumage.
Size: *L* 7 in; *W* 12 in.
Voice: call is a tinkling *tsee-titi* or *zoot;* flight song is a long series of tinkling, twittered whistles.
Status: common in open fields.
Habitat: open areas, including pastures, native prairie, cultivated or sparsely vegetated fields, golf courses, airfields and tundra.

Similar Birds

Lapland Longspur

American Pipit

Snow Bunting

small black "horns"
(rarely raised)

black line under eye
extends from bill to cheek

♂

black breast
band

dark tail with white
outer tail feathers

Nesting: on the ground; in a shallow scrape lined with grass, plant fibers and roots; brown-blotched, gray to greenish white eggs are 1 x ⅝ in; female incubates 3–4 eggs for 10–12 days.

Did You Know?

In winter, Horned Larks often flock with Lapland Longspurs and Snow Buntings in farmers' fields or at beaches.

Look For

This bird's dark tail contrasts with its light brown body and belly. Look for this feature to spot the Horned Lark in its open-country habitat.

Purple Martin
Progne subis

Purple Martins previously nested in natural tree hollows and in cliff crevices but now have virtually abandoned these in favor of human-made housing. These large swallows will entertain you throughout spring and summer if you set up a luxurious "condo complex" for them. Martin adults spiral around their accommodations in pursuit of flying insects, while their young perch clumsily at the cavity openings. To avoid the invasion of aggressive House Sparrows or European Starlings, it is essential for martin condos to be cleaned out and closed up after each nesting season.

Other ID: pointed wings; small bill.
Female: brownish above; sooty gray underparts.
Size: *L* 7–8 in; *W* 18 in.
Voice: rich, fluty, robinlike *pew-pew*, often heard in flight.
Status: uncommon and local.
Habitat: semi-open areas, often near water.

Similar Birds

European Starling
(p. 178)

Northern Rough-winged Swallow

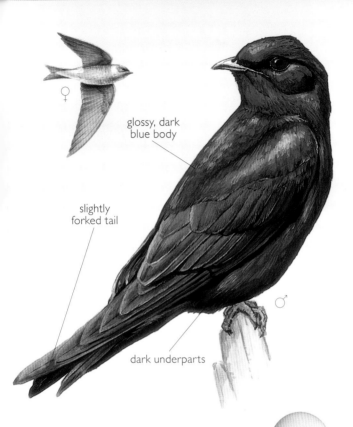

glossy, dark
blue body

slightly
forked tail

dark underparts

♀

♂

Nesting: communal; in a human-made bird-house or a hollowed-out gourd; nest is made of feathers, grass and mud; white eggs are 1 x ⅝ in; female incubates 4–5 eggs for 15–18 days.

Did You Know?

Over the last half-century Purple Martin numbers have declined in Indiana.

Look For

Purple Martins are attracted to martin condo complexes erected in open areas, high on a pole and near a body of water.

Tree Swallow
Tachycineta bicolor

Tree Swallows, our most common summer swallows, are often seen perched beside their fence-post nest boxes. When conditions are favorable, these busy birds are known to return to their young 10 to 20 times per hour (about 140 to 300 times a day!). This nearly ceaseless activity provides observers with plenty of opportunities to watch and photograph these birds in action. • In the evening and during light rains, small groups of foraging Tree Swallows sail gracefully above rivers and wetlands, catching stoneflies, mayflies and caddisflies.

Other ID: white underparts; no white on cheek. *Female:* slightly duller. *Immature:* brown above; white below. *In flight:* long, pointed wings.
Size: L 5½ in; W 14½ in.
Voice: alarm call is a metallic, buzzy *klweet*. *Male:* song is a liquid, chattering twitter.
Status: common.
Habitat: open areas, fencelines with bluebird nest boxes and fringes of open woodlands, especially near water.

Similar Birds

Northern Rough-
winged Swallow

Bank Swallow

Eastern Kingbird
(p. 134)

iridescent, dark blue or green head and upperparts

small bill

shallowly forked tail

Nesting: in a tree cavity or nest box lined with weeds, grass and feathers; white eggs are ¾ x ½ in; female incubates 4–6 eggs for up to 19 days.

Did You Know?

Tree Swallows often nest in the boxes prepared for Eastern Bluebirds. When they leave the nest to forage, they usually cover the eggs with feathers.

Look For

In the bright sunshine, the back of the Tree Swallow appears blue; prior to fall migration the back appears green.

Barn Swallow
Hirundo rustica

When you encounter this bird, you might first notice its distinctive, deeply forked tail—or you might just find yourself repeatedly ducking to avoid the dives of a protective parent. Barn Swallows once nested on cliffs, but they are now found more frequently nesting on barns, boat-houses and under bridges and house eaves. The messy young and aggressive parents unfortunately sometimes motivate people to remove nests just as nesting season is beginning, but this bird's close association with humans allows us to observe the normally secretive reproductive cycle of birds.

Other ID: blue-black upperparts; long, pointed wings.
Size: *L* 7 in; *W* 15 in.
Voice: continuous, twittering chatter: *zip-zip-zip* or *kvick-kvick*.
Status: common.
Habitat: open rural and urban areas where bridges, culverts and buildings are found near water.

Similar Birds

Cliff Swallow

Look For

Barn Swallows roll mud into small balls and build their nests one mouthful of mud at a time.

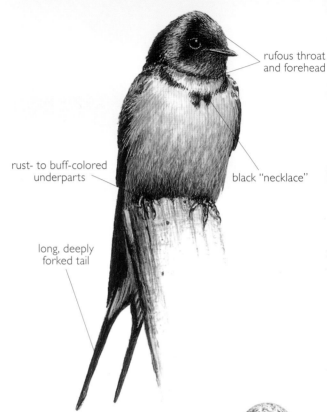

rufous throat and forehead

rust- to buff-colored underparts

black "necklace"

long, deeply forked tail

Nesting: singly or in small, loose colonies; on a human-made structure under an overhang; half or full cup nest is made of mud, grass and straw; brown-spotted, white eggs are ¾ x ½ in; pair incubates 4–7 eggs for 13–17 days.

Did You Know?

The Barn Swallow is a natural pest controller, feeding on insects that are often troublesome or harmful to crops and livestock, including horseflies, wasps and ants. Some farmers actually encourage Barn Swallows to nest on their properties by erecting narrow, wooden ledges on which the birds can build their nests.

Carolina Chickadee
Poecile carolinensis

Fidgety, friendly Carolina Chickadees are familiar to anyone in southern Indiana with a backyard feeder well stocked with sunflower seeds and peanut butter. Like some woodpeckers and nuthatches, the Carolina Chickadee will hoard food for later in the season when food may become scarce. • It's hard to imagine a chickadee using its tiny bill to excavate a nesting cavity, but come breeding season, this energetic little bird can be found hammering out a hollow in a rotting tree. • Outside of breeding season, chickadees often forage in mixed-species flocks with titmice, warblers, vireos, kinglets, nuthatches, creepers and small woodpeckers.

Other ID: white cheeks; white underparts and buffy flanks.
Size: L 4¾ in; W 7½ in.
Voice: whistling song has 4 clear notes sounding like *fee-bee fee-bay*.
Status: common in the southern half of the state.
Habitat: deciduous and mixed woods, riparian woodlands, groves and isolated shade trees; frequents urban areas.

Similar Birds

Black-capped
Chickadee

Red-breasted
Nuthatch

Blackpoll Warbler

black cap and "bib"

gray upperparts
and secondaries

Nesting: excavates or enlarges a tree cavity; may also use a nest box; cavity is lined with soft material; white eggs, marked with reddish brown, are 9/16 x 7/16 in; female incubates 5–8 eggs for 11–14 days.

Did You Know?

Chickadee flocks are often made up of close family members that vigorously defend the same territory for many generations.

Look For

These agile birds will sometimes hang upside down to grab insects and berries that other birds may not be able to reach.

Tufted Titmouse
Baeolophus bicolor

This bird's amusing feeding antics and insatiable appetite keep curious observers entertained at bird feeders. Grasping a sunflower seed with its tiny feet, the dexterous Tufted Titmouse will strike its dainty bill repeatedly against the hard outer coating to expose the inner core. • A breeding pair of Tufted Titmice will maintain their bond throughout the year, even when joining small, mixed flocks for the cold winter months.

Other ID: white underparts; pale face.
Size: *L* 6–6½ in; *W* 10 in.
Voice: noisy, scolding call, like that of a chickadee; song is a whistled *peter peter* or *peter peter peter.*
Status: common.
Habitat: deciduous woodlands, groves and suburban parks with large, mature trees.

Look For

Easily identified by its gray crest and upperparts and black forehead, the Tufted Titmouse can often be seen at feeders. Titmice always choose the largest sunflower seeds available to them, and during winter, they often cache food in bark crevices.

black
forehead

gray crest and
upperparts

buffy flanks

Nesting: in a natural cavity or woodpecker cavity lined with soft vegetation, moss and animal hair; heavily spotted, white eggs are ⅝ x ½ in; female incubates 5–6 eggs for 12–14 days.

Did You Know?

The titmouse family bond is so strong that the young from one breeding season will often stay with their parents long enough to help them with nesting and feeding duties the following year. Nesting titmice search for soft nest lining material in late winter and may accept an offering of the hair that has accumulated in your hairbrush.

White-breasted Nuthatch

Sitta carolinensis

Its upside-down antics and a noisy, nasal call make the White-breasted Nuthatch a favorite among novice birders. Whether you spot this black-capped bullet spiraling headfirst down a tree or clinging to the underside of a branch in search of invertebrates, the nuthatch's odd behavior deserves a second glance. • Comparing the White-breasted Nuthatch to the Carolina Chickadee, both regular visitors to backyard feeders, is a perfect starting point for introductory birding. While both have dark crowns and gray backs, the nuthatch's foraging behavior and undulating flight pattern are distinctive.

Other ID: white underparts; white face; straight bill; short legs. *Female:* dark gray cap.
Size: L 5½–6 in; W 11 in.
Voice: song is a fast, nasal *yank-hank yank-hank* calls include *ha-ha-ha ha-ha-ha, ank ank* and *ip*.
Status: common.
Habitat: mixedwood forests, woodlots and backyards.

Similar Birds

Red-breasted Nuthatch

Carolina Chickadee (p. 150)

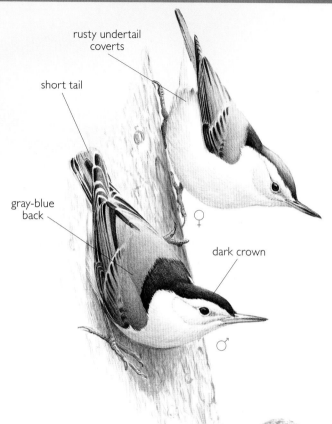

rusty undertail coverts

short tail

gray-blue back

dark crown

♀

♂

Nesting: in a natural cavity or an abandoned woodpecker nest; female lines the cavity with soft material; white eggs, speckled with brown, are ¾ x ⁹⁄₁₆ in; female incubates 5–8 eggs for 12–14 days.

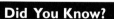

Did You Know?

This bird will wedge seeds and nuts into crevices and hack them open with its bill—hence the name "nuthatch."

Look For

Nuthatches grasp the tree through foot power alone, unlike woodpeckers, which use their tails to brace themselves against tree trunks.

Brown Creeper
Certhia americana

The cryptic Brown Creeper is never easy to find, often going unnoticed until a flake of bark suddenly takes the shape of a bird. A frightened creeper will freeze and flatten itself against a tree trunk, becoming nearly invisible. • The Brown Creeper uses its long, stiff tail feathers to prop itself up while climbing vertical tree trunks and uses its long, curved claws to grip the trunk. When it reaches the upper branches, it flies down to the base of a neighboring tree to begin another foraging ascent.

Other ID: brown upperparts with buffy white streaks; white underparts; rufous rump.
Size: *L* 5–5½ in; *W* 7½ in.
Voice: song is a faint, high-pitched *trees-trees-trees see the trees;* call is a high *tseee.*
Status: common.
Habitat: mature, mostly coniferous forests and woodlands, especially in wet areas with large, dead trees; also found near bogs.

Look For

In winter, large numbers of Brown Creepers forage on the big cottonwood trees along the Wabash River near Lafayette. They may also be seen occasionally at seed and suet feeders in backyards in winter.

downcurved bill

white eyebrow

long, pointed tail feathers

Nesting: a locally uncommon breeder in Indiana; under loose bark; nest of grass and conifer needles is woven together with spider silk; brown-spotted, whitish eggs are ⅝ x ½ in; female incubates 5–6 eggs for 14–17 days.

Did You Know?

This bird's nest is as inconspicuous as the bird itself. The nest is generally built between a piece of peeling bark and the trunk of a dead or dying tree, at least 40 feet up. Occasionally Brown Creepers also roost behind loose bark in the winter to keep warm.

Carolina Wren
Thryothorus ludovicianus

The energetic and cheerful Carolina Wren
can be shy and retiring, often hiding deep
inside dense shrubbery, so you will have to listen
for its impressive song. Pairs perform lively
"duets" at any time of day and in any season. The
duet often begins with introductory chatter by the
female, followed by innumerable ringing variations of *tea-kettle tea-kettle tea-kettle tea* from her
mate. • Carolina Wrens readily nest in the brushy
thickets of an overgrown backyard or in an
obscure nook in a house or barn. If conditions are
favorable, two broods may be raised in a single
season.

Other ID: rusty cheek; white throat; longish,
slightly downcurved bill; tail is rather long for
a wren.
Size: *L* 5½ in; *W* 7½ in.
Voice: loud, repetitious *tea-kettle tea-kettle
tea-kettle tea* may be heard at any time of day
or year; female often chatters while male sings.
Status: common.
Habitat: dense forest undergrowth, especially
shrubby tangles and thickets.

Similar Birds

House Wren
(p. 160)

Marsh Wren

rich brown upperparts, including nape and crown

bold white eyebrow

rich, buff-colored underparts

Nesting: in a nest box or natural or artificial cavity; nest is lined with soft materials, including a shed snakeskin at the entrance; brown-blotched, white eggs are ¾ x ⁹⁄₁₆ in; female incubates 4–5 eggs for 12–16 days.

Did You Know?

Frigid temperatures, such as those in the winters of 1976 and 1977, can decimate an otherwise healthy population, but numbers can rebound nicely.

Look For

A nesting Carolina Wren will not hesitate to give intruders a severe scolding but remains hidden all the while.

House Wren
Troglodytes aedon

The bland, nondescript plumage of this suburban and city park dweller can be overlooked until you hear it sing a seemingly unending song in one breath. The voice of the House Wren sounds like an old-fashioned sewing machine. • This wren can be very aggressive toward other species that nest in its territory, puncturing and tossing eggs from other bird's nests. A House Wren often builds many nests, which later serve as decoys or "dummy" nests to fool potential enemies.

Other ID: whitish throat; brown upperparts; whitish to buff underparts; faintly barred flanks.
Size: *L* 4½–5 in; W 6 in.
Voice: smooth, running, bubbly warble: *tsi-tsi-tsi-tsi oodle-oodle-oodle-oodle*.
Status: common, especially in suburban areas.
Habitat: thickets and shrubby openings in or at the edge of deciduous or mixed woodlands; often in shrubs and thickets near buildings.

Similar Birds

Carolina Wren
(p. 158)

Winter Wren

short, upraised tail is finely barred with black

fine, dark barring on upperwings and lower back

faint, pale eyebrow and eye ring

Nesting: in a natural or artificial cavity or abandoned woodpecker nest; nest of sticks and grass is lined with feathers and fur; heavily marked, white eggs are ⅝ x ½ in; female incubates 6–8 eggs for 12–15 days.

Did You Know?

This bird has the largest range of any New World passerine, stretching from Canada to southern South America.

Look For

Like all wrens, the House Wren usually carries its short tail raised upward.

Ruby-crowned Kinglet

Regulus calendula

This kinglet's familiar voice echoes through our forests in April as it migrates through our state to breeding grounds in the boreal forest. Not only does the male Ruby-crowned Kinglet possess a loud, complex, warbling song to bring him some attention, but he also wears a nifty red crest to help attract a mate and defend his territory in spring. Unfortunately, his distinctive crown is only visible in the breeding season, leaving him with just his dull olive green plumage for the rest of the year.

Other ID: olive green upperparts; dark wings; whitish to yellowish underparts; flicks its wings.
Size: *L* 4 in; *W* 7½ in.
Voice: Male: song is an accelerating and rising *tea-tea-tea-tew-tew-tew look-at-Me, look-at-Me, look-at-Me.*
Status: common during spring and fall migrations.
Habitat: mixed woodlands and pure coniferous forests, especially with spruce; often near wet forest openings and edges.

Similar Birds

Golden-crowned Kinglet

Blue-gray Gnatcatcher (p. 164)

Orange-crowned Warbler

bold, broken eye ring

2 white wing bars

male's small, red crown is usually hidden

♀

♂

short, dark tail

Nesting: does not nest in Indiana; nests in Alaska, Canada and the northern and western U.S.; usually in a conifer; female builds a hanging nest of lichen, twigs and leaves; brown-spotted, white to pale buff eggs are ½ x ⅜ in; female incubates 7–8 eggs for 13–14 days.

Did You Know?

Females can lay an impressively large clutch with up to 12 eggs, which together often weigh as much as the bird that laid them!

Look For

Watch for this bird's hovering technique and wing-flicking behavior to distinguish it from similar-looking flycatchers.

Blue-gray Gnatcatcher
Polioptila caerulea

The fidgety Blue-gray Gnatcatcher is constantly on the move. This woodland inhabitant holds its tail upward like a wren and issues a quiet, banjolike twang while flitting restlessly from shrub to shrub.
• Gnatcatcher pairs remain close once a bond is established, and both parents share the responsibilities of nest-building, incubation and raising the young. Like most songbirds, Blue-gray Gnatcatchers mature quickly and will fly as far as South America within months of hatching.
• The scientific name *Polioptila* means "gray feather," while *caerulea* means "blue."

Other ID: pale gray underparts; black uppertail. *Breeding male:* darker upperparts; black border on side of forecrown.
Size: *L* 4½ in; *W* 6 in.
Voice: song is a faint, airy *puree;* call is a banjolike, high-pitched twang.
Status: common.
Habitat: deciduous woodlands along streams, ponds, lakes and swamps; also in orchards and shrubby tangles along woodland edges and oak savannas.

Similar Birds

Golden-crowned Kinglet

Ruby-crowned Kinglet (p. 162)

Carolina Chickadee (p. 158)

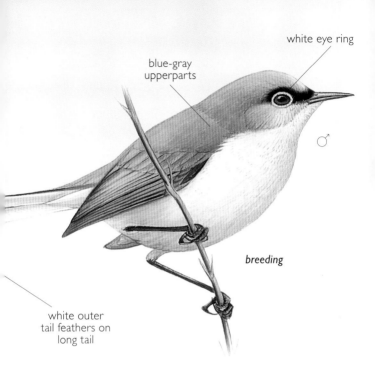

white eye ring

blue-gray
upperparts

♂

breeding

white outer
tail feathers on
long tail

Nesting: cup nest is made of plant fibers and
bark chips and is decorated with lichens; nest
is lined with soft hair and plants; brown-
spotted, pale bluish white eggs are 9/16 x 7/16 in;
female incubates 3–5 eggs for 11–15 days.

Did You Know?

Although this bird
undoubtedly eats gnats,
this food item is only a
small part of its insectivo-
rous diet.

Look For

Foraging gnatcatchers often
flash their white outer tail
feathers, an action that
reflects light and may scare
insects into flight.

Eastern Bluebird
Sialia sialis

The Eastern Bluebird's enticing colors are like those of a warm setting sun against a deep blue sky. • This cavity nester's survival has been put to the test—populations have declined in the presence of the competitive, introduced House Sparrow and European Starling. The removal of standing dead trees has also diminished nest site availability. Thankfully, bluebird enthusiasts and organizations have developed "bluebird trails," mounting nest boxes on fence posts along highways and rural roads, allowing Eastern Bluebird numbers to gradually recover.

Other ID: dark bill; dark legs. *Female:* thin, white eye ring; gray-brown head and back are tinged with blue; blue wings and tail; paler chestnut underparts.
Size: *L* 7 in; *W* 13 in.
Voice: song is a rich, warbling *turr, turr-lee, turr-lee;* call is a chittering *pew.*
Status: common.
Habitat: cropland fencelines, meadows, pastures, fallow and abandoned fields; forest clearings and edges; golf courses, large lawns and cemeteries.

Similar Birds

Indigo Bunting
(p. 210)

Look For

The Eastern Bluebird hunts insects from an elevated perch. It also feeds on berries and is especially attracted to wild grapes, sumac and currants.

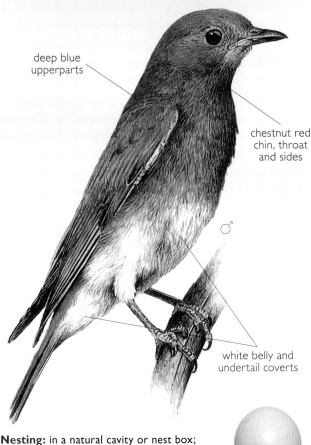

deep blue
upperparts

chestnut red
chin, throat
and sides

♂

white belly and
undertail coverts

Nesting: in a natural cavity or nest box;
female builds a cup nest of grass, weed stems
and small twigs; pale blue eggs are ⅞ x ⅝ in;
female incubates 4–5 eggs for 13–16 days.

Did You Know?

It is the structure of the feathers, not any pigmentation, that
is responsible for the intense blue of this bird's plumage. The
feather color is really black, but the feather scatters light to
give the appearance of blue, which is similar to how light is
scattered off of small molecules in the atmosphere to give the
sky its blue color.

Wood Thrush
Hylocichla mustelina

The loud, warbled notes of the Wood Thrush once resounded through our woodlands, but forest fragmentation and urban sprawl have eliminated much of this bird's nesting habitat. Broken forests and diminutive woodlots have allowed the invasion of common, open-area predators and parasites, such as raccoons, skunks, crows, jays and cowbirds. Traditionally, these predators had little access to nests that were hidden deep within vast hardwood forests. Many forests that have been urbanized or developed for agriculture now host families of American Robins rather than the once-prominent Wood Thrushes.

Other ID: plump body; streaked cheeks; brown wings, rump and tail.
Size: *L* 8 in; *W* 13 in.
Voice: *Male:* bell-like phrases of 3–5 notes, with each note at a different pitch and followed by a trill: *Will you live with me? Way up high in a tree, I'll come right down and…seeee!;* calls include a *pit pit* and *bweebeebeep.*
Status: common.
Habitat: moist, mature and preferably undisturbed deciduous woodlands and mixed forests.

Similar Birds

Swainson's Thrush

Veery

Hermit Thrush

bold, white eye ring

rusty head and back

large, black spots on white breast, sides and flanks

Nesting: low in a fork of a deciduous tree; female builds a bulky cup nest of vegetation, held together with mud and lined with softer materials; eggs are 1 x ¾ in; female incubates 3–4 pale, greenish blue eggs for 13–14 days.

Did You Know?

Henry David Thoreau considered the Wood Thrush's song to be the most beautiful. The male can even sing two notes at once!

Look For

Wood Thrushes forage on the ground or glean vegetation for insects and other invertebrates.

American Robin
Turdus migratorius

Come March, the familiar song of the American Robin may wake you early if you are a light sleeper. This abundant bird adapts easily to urban areas and often works from dawn until after dusk when there is a nest to be built or hungry, young mouths to feed. • The robin's bright red belly contrasts with its dark head and wings, making this bird easy to identify. • In winter, fruit trees may attract flocks of robins, which gather to drink the fermenting fruit's intoxicating juices.

Other ID: incomplete white eye ring; gray-brown back; white undertail coverts.
Size: *L* 10 in; *W* 17 in.
Voice: song is an evenly spaced warble: *cheerily cheer-up cheerio;* call is a rapid *tut-tut-tut.*
Status: common.
Habitat: *Breeding:* residential lawns and gardens, pastures, urban parks, broken forests, bogs and river shorelines. *Winter:* near fruit-bearing trees and springs.

Look For

A hunting robin with its head tilted to the side isn't listening for prey—it is actually looking for movements in the soil. It tilts its head to the side because its eyes are located on the sides of its head.

black head

white throat is streaked with black

dark gray head

black-tipped, yellow bill

♂ ♀

brick red breast is darker on male

Nesting: in a tree or shrub; cup nest is built of grass, moss, bark and mud; light blue eggs are 1⅛ x ¾ in; female incubates 4 eggs for 11–16 days; raises up to 3 broods per year.

Did You Know?

American Robins do not use nest boxes; they prefer platforms for their nests. Robins usually raise two broods per year, and the male cares for the fledglings from the first brood while the female incubates the second clutch of eggs.

Gray Catbird
Dumetella carolinensis

The Gray Catbird is an accomplished mimic that may fool you as it shuffles through underbrush and dense riparian shrubs, calling its catlike meow. Its mimicking talents are further enhanced by its ability to sing two notes at once, using each side of its syrinx individually.

• The Gray Catbird will vigilantly defend its territory against sparrows, robins, cowbirds and other intruders. It will destroy the eggs and nestlings of other songbirds and will take on an intense defensive posture if approached, screaming and even attempting to hit an intruder.

Other ID: dark gray overall; black eyes, bill and legs.
Size: *L* 8½–9 in; *W* 11 in.
Voice: calls include a catlike *meoww* and a harsh *check-check;* song is a variety of warbles, squeaks and mimicked phrases interspersed with a *mew* call.
Status: very common and widespread.
Habitat: dense thickets, brambles, shrubby or brushy areas and hedgerows, often near water.

Similar Birds

Northern Mockingbird
(p. 174)

Look For

If you catch a glimpse of this bird during the breeding season, watch the male raise his long, slender tail to show off his rust-colored undertail coverts.

black cap

long tail is dark
gray to black

chestnut undertail
coverts

Nesting: in a dense shrub or thicket; bulky
cup nest is made of twigs, leaves and grass;
greenish blue eggs are ⅞ x ⅝ in; female
incubates 4 eggs for 12–15 days.

Did You Know?

The watchful female Gray Catbird can recognize a Brown-
headed Cowbird egg as different from her own and will
remove it from her nest. Only a dozen or so of the over 140
species of birds parasitized by the Brown-headed Cowbird in
North America are known to remove cowbird eggs from
their nests.

Northern Mockingbird
Mimus polyglottos

The Northern Mockingbird has an amazing vocal repertoire that includes over 400 different song types, which it belts out incessantly throughout the breeding season, serenading into the night during a full moon. Mockingbirds can imitate almost anything. In some instances, they replicate notes so accurately that even computerized sound analysis is unable to detect the difference between the original source and the mockingbird's imitation.

Other ID: gray upperparts; 2 thin, white wing bars; light gray underparts.
Size: *L* 10 in; *W* 14 in.
Voice: song is a medley of mimicked phrases, with the phrases often repeated 3 times or more; calls include a harsh *chair* and *chewk*.
Status: generally common, but rare near Lake Michigan.
Habitat: hedges, suburban gardens and orchard margins with an abundance of available fruit; hedgerows of multiflora roses are especially important in winter.

Similar Birds

Loggerhead Shrike

Northern Shrike

Gray Catbird
(p. 172)

long, dark tail with white outer tail feathers

thin, dark eye line

dark wings

Nesting: often in a small shrub or small tree; cup nest is built with twigs and plants; brown-blotched, bluish gray to greenish eggs are 1 x ⅝ in; female incubates 3–4 eggs for 12–13 days.

Did You Know?

The scientific name *polyglottos* is Greek for "many tongues" and refers to this bird's ability to mimic a wide variety of sounds.

Look For

The Northern Mockingbird's energetic territorial dance is delightful to watch, as males square off in what appears to be a swordless fencing duel.

Brown Thrasher
Toxostoma rufum

The Brown Thrasher shares the streaked breast of a thrush and the long tail of a catbird, but it has a temper all its own. Because it nests close to the ground, the Brown Thrasher defends its nest with a vengeance, attacking snakes and other nest robbers sometimes to the point of drawing blood. • Biologists have estimated that the male Brown Thrasher is capable of producing up to 3000 distinctive song phrases—the most extensive vocal repertoire of any North American bird.

Other ID: reddish brown upperparts; long, rufous tail; orange-yellow eyes.
Size: *L* 11½ in; *W* 13 in.
Voice: sings a large variety of phrases, with each phrase usually repeated twice: *dig-it dig-it, hoe-it hoe-it, pull-it-up pull-it-up;* calls include a loud crackling note, a harsh *shuck*, a soft *churr* or a whistled, 3-note *pit-cher-ee*.
Status: common.
Habitat: dense shrubs and thickets, overgrown pastures, woodland edges and brushy areas, rarely close to urban areas.

Look For

The Brown Thrasher often remains concealed in shrubby understory habitat as it probes through the leaf litter and soil with its long bill expertly moving from side to side. You might catch only a flash of rufous as the Brown Thrasher flies from one thicket to another.

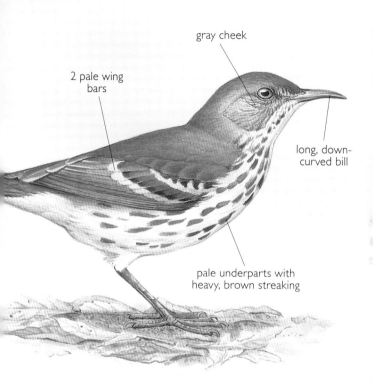

gray cheek

2 pale wing bars

long, down-curved bill

pale underparts with heavy, brown streaking

Nesting: usually in a low shrub; often on the ground; cup nest, made of grass, twigs and leaves, is lined with vegetation; pale blue eggs, dotted with reddish brown are 1 x ¾ in; pair incubates 4 eggs for 11–14 days.

Did You Know?

Though not threatened or endangered, Brown Thrashers are suffering degradation of their habitat across North America. Fencing shrubby, wooded areas bordering wetlands and streams can prevent cattle from devastating thrasher nesting habitat.

European Starling
Sturnus vulgaris

The European Starling did not hesitate to make itself known across North America after being released in New York's Central Park in 1890 and 1891. It took fewer than 30 years for these birds to extend their range to Indiana—our first sighting was in 1919. This highly adaptable bird not only took over the nest sites of native cavity nesters, such as Tree Swallows and Red-headed Woodpeckers, but it also learned to mimic the sounds of Killdeers, Red-tailed Hawks, Soras and meadowlarks. • Look for European Starlings in massive evening roosts under bridges or on buildings in late summer and through winter.

Other ID: dark eyes; short, squared tail.
Nonbreeding: feather tips are heavily spotted with white and buff; dull yellow bill.
Size: L 8½ in; W 16 in.
Voice: variety of whistles, squeaks and gurgles; imitates other birds.
Status: abundant.
Habitat: *Breeding:* cities, towns, residential areas, farmyards, woodland fringes and clearings. *Winter:* near feedlots and pastures.

Similar Birds

Brewer's Blackbird

Brown-headed Cowbird
(p. 218)

Rusty Blackbird

iridescent, purple-black
head, neck and breast

glossy, green back
with buffy spots

yellow bill

greenish black
underparts

breeding

Nesting: in an abandoned woodpecker cavity, natural cavity or nest box; nest is made of grass, twigs and straw; bluish to greenish white eggs are $1\frac{1}{8}$ x $\frac{7}{8}$ in; female incubates 4–6 eggs for 12–14 days.

Did You Know?

Starlings were brought to New York as part of a local group's plan to introduce all the birds mentioned in William Shakespeare's writings.

Look For

It can be confused for a blackbird, but note the European Starling's shorter tail and bright yellow bill in breeding plumage.

Cedar Waxwing
Bombycilla cedrorum

With its black mask and slick hairdo, the Cedar Waxwing has a heroic look. This bird's splendid personality is reflected in its amusing antics after it gorges on fermented berries and in its gentle courtship dance. To court a mate, the gentlemanly male hops toward a female and offers her a berry. The female accepts the berry and hops away, then stops and hops back toward the male to offer him the berry in return. • If a bird's crop is full and it is unable to eat any more, it will continue to pluck fruit and pass it down the line like a bucket brigade, until the fruit is gulped down by a still-hungry bird.

Other ID: brown upperparts; yellow wash on belly; gray rump; white undertail coverts.
Size: *L* 7 in; *W* 12 in.
Voice: faint, high-pitched, trilled whistle: *tseee-tseee-tseee.*
Status: common but nomadic.
Habitat: wooded residential parks and gardens, overgrown fields, forest edges, second-growth, riparian and open woodlands; often near fruit trees and water.

Similar Birds

Bohemian Waxwing

Look For

The Bohemian Waxwing is a rare winter visitor that is seen only occasionally in Indiana. It has rufous undertail coverts and more rufous on its face.

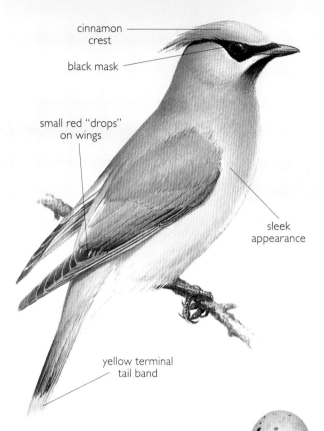

cinnamon crest

black mask

small red "drops" on wings

sleek appearance

yellow terminal tail band

Nesting: in a tree or shrub; cup nest is made of twigs, moss and lichen; darkly spotted, bluish to gray eggs are ⅞ x ⅝ in; female incubates 3–5 eggs for 12–16 days.

Did You Know?

Cedar Waxwings are very social birds, often seen in flocks moving from one berry-laden tree or shrub to another. In late May, impressive flocks, often numbering into the thousands, occur along the Lake Michigan shoreline; indeed, 13,800 were counted on May 22, 2004.

Yellow Warbler
Dendroica petechia

The Yellow Warbler is often parasitized by the Brown-headed Cowbird and can recognize cowbird eggs, but rather than tossing them out, this warbler will build another nest overtop the old eggs or abandon the nest completely. Occasionally, cowbirds strike repeatedly—a five-story nest was once found! • The widely distributed Yellow Warbler arrives in early May, flitting from branch to branch in search of juicy caterpillars, aphids and beetles and singing its *sweet-sweet* song. Most Yellow Warblers leave Indiana in late summer.
• The Yellow Warbler is often mistakenly called "Wild Canary."

Other ID: bright yellow body; yellow edgings on flight feathers; black bill and eyes. *Female:* may have faint, red breast streaks.
Size: *L* 5 in; *W* 8 in.
Voice: song is a fast, frequently repeated *sweet-sweet-sweet summer sweet.*
Status: common.
Habitat: moist, open woodlands, dense scrub, scrubby meadows, second-growth woodlands, riparian woods and urban parks and gardens.

Similar Birds

Orange-crowned Warbler

American Goldfinch (p. 226)

Wilson's Warbler

♀

♂

bright yellow
highlights on dark
olive yellow tail
and wings

red breast
streaks

Nesting: in a deciduous tree or shrub;
female builds a cup nest of grass, weeds and
shredded bark; darkly speckled, greenish white
eggs are ⅝ x ½ in; female incubates 4–5 eggs
for 11–12 days.

Did You Know?

The Yellow Warbler has
an amazing geographical
range. It is found throughout North America and
on islands in Central and
South America.

Look For

These widespread habitat
generalists favor moist habitats and brushy thickets for
breeding but may visit
orchards and gardens during
migration.

Yellow-rumped Warbler

Dendroica coronata

The Yellow-rumped Warbler is the most abundant and widespread wood-warbler in North America. Apple, juniper and sumac trees laden with fruit attract this bird in winter. • This species comes in two forms: the common, white-throated "Myrtle Warbler" of the East, and the yellow-throated "Audubon's Warbler" of the West, which is extremely rare in Indiana. Although Myrtles do not breed in our state, they are commonly seen during migration.

Other ID: *Breeding Myrtle Warbler male:* white throat; yellow rump and shoulder patch; yellow cap; black streaking on breast. *Breeding Myrtle Warbler female:* similar to breeding male but lacks yellow cap.
Size: L 5½ in; W 9¼ in.
Voice: male's song is a brief, variable, bubbling *warble*, rising or falling at the end; call is a sharp *chip* or *chet*.
Status: abundant during migration; uncommon in southern Indiana in winter.
Habitat: a variety of well-vegetated habitats in lowlands, especially in wax myrtle thickets.

Similar Birds

Black-throated
Green Warbler

Cape May Warbler

Magnolia Warbler

yellow throat

2 white wing bars

yellow shoulder patch

♂

yellow rump

nonbreeding

"Audubon's Warbler"

streaked breast

♀

Nesting: does not nest in Indiana; nests in Canada and in the western and northern U.S.; in a crotch or on a horizontal limb of a conifer; cup nest is made of vegetation and spider silk; brown-blotched, buff-colored eggs are ⅝ x ½ in; female incubates 4–5 eggs for up to 13 days.

Did You Know?

This small warbler's habit of flitting near buildings to snatch spiders from their webs has earned it the nickname "Spider Bird."

Look For

Small puddles that form during or after rains often attract warblers, allowing a glimpse of these secretive birds.

Blackburnian Warbler
Dendroica fusca

The colorful Blackburnian Warbler's fiery orange throat glows ablaze in spring. Widely regarded as one of the most beautiful warblers in North America, the Blackburnian Warbler stays hidden in the upper canopy. • To coexist and reduce competition for food, different species of wood-warblers forage in separate areas of a tree and use unique feeding strategies. Blackburnians have found their niche among the crowns of hardwoods, whereas other warblers restrict themselves to inner branches and tree trunks or to lower branches.

Other ID: *Breeding male:* blackish upperparts with bold whitish lines; yellowish to whitish underparts; dark streaking on sides and flanks; may show some white on outer tail feathers. *Female:* brown version of male; more yellow on upper breast and throat than male.

Size: *L* 4½–5½ in; *W* 8½ in.

Voice: song is a soft, faint, high-pitched *ptoo-too-too-too tititi zeee* or *see-me see-me see-me see-me;* call is a short *tick.*

Status: common migrant; rare summer resident.

Habitat: woodlands or areas with tall shrubs.

Similar Birds

Yellow-throated Warbler

Prairie Warbler

2 broad, black crown stripes

yellow-orange head with angular, black mask

fiery reddish orange upper breast and throat

large white wing patch

♂

♀

breeding

Nesting: high in a mature white spruce, often near the tip of a branch; cup nest is made of conifer needles, bark, twigs and grass; white eggs with brownish markings are ⅝ x ½ in; female incubates 3–5 eggs for up to 13 days.

Did You Know?

This bird's name is thought to honor the Blackburne family of England, whose members collected the type specimens for a museum.

Look For

The Blackburnian Warbler is the only warbler in North America with an orange throat.

American Redstart
Setophaga ruticilla

This bird's Latin American name, *candelita*, meaning "little torch," also describes it perfectly. Not only are the male's bright orange patches the color of a glowing flame, but the bird never ceases to flicker, even when perched. • The American Redstart flushes insects with the flash of color from its wings or tail. Then it uses its broad bill and the bristles around its mouth to capture insects. • This striking warbler is Indiana's second most common migrant warbler, behind the Yellow-rumped.

Other ID: *Male:* white belly and undertail coverts. *Female:* pale gray underparts and head.
Size: *L* 5 in; *W* 8½ in.
Voice: male's song is a highly variable series of *tseet* or *zee* notes at different pitches; call is a sharp, sweet *chip*.
Status: common in summer and during migration.
Habitat: shrubby woodland edges; open and semi-open forests with a regenerating deciduous understory; often near water; prefers alder swales and thickets in migration.

Similar Birds

Baltimore Oriole
(p. 220)

Orchard Oriole

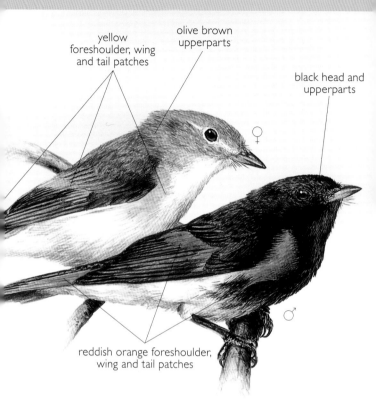

yellow foreshoulder, wing and tail patches

olive brown upperparts

black head and upperparts

♀

♂

reddish orange foreshoulder, wing and tail patches

Nesting: in a shrub or sapling; female builds open cup nest of plant down, bark shreds, grass and rootlets; brown-marked, whitish eggs are ⅝ x ½ in; female incubates 4 eggs for 11–12 days.

Did You Know?

This bird's high-pitched, lisping, trilly songs are so variable that identifying an American Redstart by song alone is a challenge to birders of all levels.

Look For

Even when an American Redstart is perched, its color-splashed tail sways rhythmically back and forth.

Ovenbird
Seiurus aurocapilla

Even the sharpest human eye will have trouble spotting the Ovenbird's immaculately concealed nest along hiking trails and bike paths. An incubating female is usually confident enough in the camouflage of her ground nest that she will choose to sit tight rather than flee in the presence of danger. Furthermore, some females have as many as three mates to call on for protection and to help feed the young. Despite these evolutionary adaptations, forest fragmentation and Brown-headed Cowbird parasitism have reduced this bird's nesting success.

Other ID: olive brown upperparts; no wing bars; white undertail coverts; pink legs.
Size: L 6 in; W 9½ in.
Voice: loud, distinctive *tea-cher tea-cher Tea-CHER Tea-CHER*, increasing in speed and volume; night song is a set of bubbly, warbled notes, often ending in *teacher-teacher;* call is a brisk *chip, cheep* or *chock*.
Status: common migrant and summer resident.
Habitat: *Breeding:* undisturbed, mature forests with a closed canopy and little understory. *In migration:* dense riparian shrubs and thickets.

Similar Birds

Northern
Waterthrush

Louisiana
Waterthrush

Wood Thrush
(p. 168)

white eye ring

rufous crown bordered by black

heavy, dark streaking on white breast, sides and flanks

Nesting: on the ground; female builds a domed, oven-shaped nest of grass, twigs, bark and dead leaves, lined with animal hair; gray-and-brown-spotted, white eggs are ¾ x ½ in; female incubates 4–5 eggs for 11–13 days.

Did You Know?

The name "Ovenbird" refers to this bird's unusual ground nest, which is the shape of a Dutch oven.

Look For

In summer, the male's loud *tea-cher* song will give away his presence as he hides among tangled shrubs or conifer branches.

Common Yellowthroat

Geothlypis trichas

The bumblebee colors of the male Common Yellowthroat's black mask and yellow throat identify this skulking wetland resident. He sings his *witchety* song from strategically chosen cattail perches that he visits in rotation, fiercely guarding his territory against the intrusion of other males. • The Common Yellowthroat is different from most wood-warblers, preferring marshlands and wet, overgrown meadows to forests. The female wears no mask and remains mostly hidden from view in thick vegetation when she tends to the nest.

Other ID: black bill; orangy legs. *Female:* no face mask; may show faint, white eye ring.
Size: L 5 in; W 7 in.
Voice: song is a clear, oscillating *witchety witchety witchety-witch;* call is a sharp *tcheck* or *tchet.*
Status: common and widespread.
Habitat: cattail marshes, sedge wetlands, riparian areas, beaver ponds and wet, over-grown meadows; sometimes dry fields.

Similar Birds

Kentucky Warbler

Mourning Warbler

Nashville Warbler

olive green to olive brown upperparts

dingy white belly

♀

broad, black mask with white upper border

♂

yellow throat, breast and undertail coverts

Nesting: on or near the ground or in a small shrub or emergent vegetation; female builds an open cup nest of weeds, grass, bark strips and moss; brown-blotched, white eggs are ⅝ x ½ in; female incubates 3–5 eggs for 12 days.

Did You Know?

Swedish biologist Carolus Linnaeus named the Common Yellowthroat in 1766, making it one of the first North American birds to be described.

Look For

Common Yellowthroats immerse themselves or roll in water, then shake off the excess water by flicking or flapping their wings.

Scarlet Tanager
Piranga olivacea

The vibrant red of a breeding male Scarlet Tanager may catch your eye in Indiana's wooded ravines and migrant stopover sites. Because this tanager is more likely to reside in forest canopies, birders tend to hear the Scarlet Tanager before they see it. Its song, a sort of slurred version of the American Robin's, is a much anticipated sound that announces the arrival of this colorful long-distance migrant. The Scarlet Tanager has the northernmost breeding grounds and longest migration route of all tanager species and is one of two tanager species that routinely nest in Indiana.

Other ID: *Female:* uniformly olive upperparts; yellow eye ring; yellow underparts; grayish brown wings. *Nonbreeding male:* similar to female.
Size: *L* 7 in; *W* 11½ in.
Voice: song is a series of 4–5 sweet, clear, whistled phrases; call is *chip-burrr* or *chip-churrr*.
Status: common in migration and during summer.
Habitat: fairly mature, upland deciduous and mixed forests.

Similar Birds

Summer Tanager

Northern Cardinal
(p. 208)

pale bill

♂

bright red body

♀

pure black
wings and tail

breeding

Nesting: high in a deciduous tree; female
builds a flimsy, shallow cup nest of grass,
weeds and twigs; brown-spotted, pale blue-
green eggs are ⅞ x ⅝ in; female incubates
2–5 eggs for 12–14 days.

Did You Know?

In Central and South
America, there are over
200 tanager species in
every color imaginable.

Look For

Scarlet Tanagers forage in the
forest understory in cold,
rainy weather, making them
easier to observe.

Eastern Towhee
Pipilo erythrophthalmus

Eastern Towhees are large, colorful members of the sparrow family that rustle about in dense undergrowth, craftily scraping back layers of dry leaves to expose the seeds, berries or insects hidden beneath. While foraging, towhees employ an unusual two-footed technique to uncover food items—a strategy that is especially important in winter when virtually all of their food is taken from the ground. • The Eastern Towhee and its western relative, the Spotted Towhee (*P. maculata*), were once grouped together as the "Rufous-sided Towhee."

Other ID: white lower breast and belly; buff undertail coverts. *In flight:* white outer tail corners.
Size: L 7–8½ in; W 10½ in.
Voice: song is 2 high, whistled notes followed by a trill: *drink your teeeee*; call is a scratchy, slurred *cheweee!* or *chewink!*
Status: common.
Habitat: along woodland edges and in shrubby, abandoned fields.

Similar Birds

Spotted Towhee

Dark-eyed Junco
(p. 206)

black back, hood and bill

brown hood and upperparts

♂

♀

rufous sides and flanks

small, white wing patch

Nesting: on the ground or low in a dense shrub; female builds a cup nest of twigs, bark strips, grass and animal hair; pale, brown-spotted, creamy eggs are ⅞ x ⅝ in; mainly the female incubates 3–4 eggs for 12–13 days.

Did You Know?

The scientific name *eryth-rophthalmus* means "red eye" in Greek, though towhees in the southeastern states may have white or orange irises.

Look For

Showy towhees are easily attracted to feeders, where they scratch on the ground for millet, oats or sunflower seeds.

American Tree Sparrow

Spizella arborea

Most of us know these rufous-capped, spot-breasted sparrows as winter visitors to agricultural fields and backyard feeders, though their numbers fluctuate depending on the year and location.
• The American Tree Sparrow's name suggests a close relationship with trees or forests, but this bird actually makes its home in treeless fields and semi-open, shrubby habitats. It breeds at or above the treeline at northern latitudes, then returns to weedy fields in southern Canada and the north-central U.S. to overwinter.

Other ID: mottled brown upperparts; notched tail; dark legs; dark upper mandible; yellow lower mandible. *Nonbreeding:* gray central crown stripe. *Juvenile:* streaky breast and head.
Size: L 6¼ in; W 9½ in.
Voice: a high, whistled *tseet-tseet* is followed by a short, sweet, musical series of slurred whistles; call is a 3-note *tsee-dle-eat*.
Status: common in winter.
Habitat: brushy thickets, roadside shrubs, semi-open fields and agricultural croplands.

Similar Birds

Chipping Sparrow

Swamp Sparrow

Field Sparrow

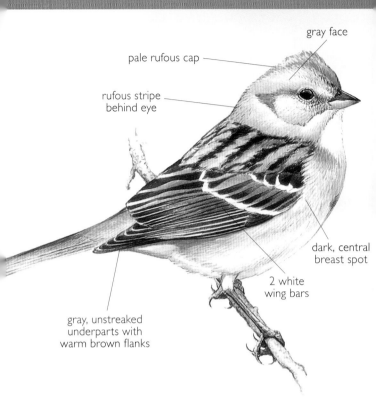

gray face

pale rufous cap

rufous stripe behind eye

dark, central breast spot

2 white wing bars

gray, unstreaked underparts with warm brown flanks

Nesting: does not nest in Indiana; nests in northern Canada and Alaska; on the ground or in a shrub; open cup nest of grass, moss, bark shreds and twigs is lined with feathers and fine grass; brown-spotted, pale greenish or bluish eggs are ⅞ x ½ in; female incubates 4–6 eggs for 11–13 days.

Did You Know?

These birds begin courtship in late winter and during spring migration, singing their bubbly, bright songs as they move northward.

Look For

These sparrows forage by scratching at the ground for seeds and are often seen in mixed flocks with Dark-eyed Juncos.

Song Sparrow
Melospiza melodia

This well-named bird is among the great singers of the bird world. When a young male Song Sparrow is only a few months old, he has already created a courtship tune of his own, having learned the basics of melody and rhythm from his father and rival males. • In winter, adaptable Song Sparrows are common throughout Indiana and inhabit woodland edges, weedy ditches and riparian thickets. They regularly visit backyard feeders, belting out their sweet, three-part song throughout the year.

Other ID: mottled brown upperparts; rounded tail tip.
Size: *L* 6–7 in; *W* 8 in.
Voice: song is 1–4 introductory notes, such as *sweet sweet sweet*, followed by a buzzy *towee*, then a short, descending trill; call is short *tsip* or *tchep*.
Status: common and widespread.
Habitat: willow shrublands, riparian thickets, forest openings and pastures; often near water.

Similar Birds

Savannah Sparrow

Fox Sparrow

Lincoln's Sparrow

dark crown with pale central stripe

grayish face

brown line behind eye

white jaw line with dark "mustache" stripes

heavy brown streaks converge at central breast spot

Nesting: usually on the ground or in a low shrub; female builds an open cup nest of grass, weeds and bark strips; brown-blotched, greenish white eggs are ⅞ x ⅝ in; female incubates 3–5 eggs for 12–14 days.

Did You Know?

Though female songbirds are not usually vocal, the female Song Sparrow will occasionally sing a tune of her own.

Look For

The Song Sparrow pumps its long, rounded tail in flight. It also often issues a high-pitched *seet* flight call.

White-throated Sparrow
Zonotrichia albicollis

The White-throated Sparrow is Indiana's most abundant sparrow. Its distinctive song makes it one of the easiest sparrows to learn and identify. Its familiar appearance, with a bold white throat and a striped crown, is often confused with the White-crowned Sparrow, but White-throats usually stick to forested woodlands, whereas White-crowns prefer open, bushy habitats and farmlands. • Two color morphs are common: one has black and white stripes on the head, the other has brown and tan stripes. Each morph almost always breeds with the opposite color morph.

Other ID: gray cheek; black eye line; unstreaked, gray underparts; mottled brown upperparts.
Size: L 6½–7½ in; W 9 in.
Voice: variable song is a clear, whistled *Old Sam Peabody, Peabody, Peabody;* call is a sharp *chink.*
Status: common to abundant, especially during migration.
Habitat: woodlots, wooded parks and riparian brush.

Similar Birds

White-crowned Sparrow
(p. 204)

Swamp Sparrow

black and white (or brown and tan) stripes on head

yellow lores

grayish bill

white throat

Nesting: on or near the ground, often concealed by a low shrub or fallen log; open cup nest of grass and plant material is lined with fine grass and hair; bluish, spotted eggs are ⅞ x ⁹⁄₁₆ in; female incubates 4–5 eggs for 11–14 days.

Did You Know?

Zonotrichia means "hair-like," a reference to the striped heads of birds in this genus.

Look For

During migration, White-throated Sparrows forage mostly on the ground. They kick aside the leaf litter and pounce on insects that they find underneath.

White-crowned Sparrow

Zonotrichia leucophrys

In winter, large, bold and smartly patterned White-crowned Sparrows brighten brushy hedge-rows, overgrown fields and riparian areas. They flit between shrubs, picking seeds from leaf litter and sounding their surprisingly loud, high-pitched *seep* notes. During migration, these sparrows may visit bird feeders stocked with cracked corn. • Several different races of the White-crowned Sparrow occur in North America, so not all birds sound alike, but they all give a slight variation of *I-I-I-got-to-go-wee-wee-now!* Their song can be heard in late winter and spring in Indiana.

Other ID: a large sparrow; streaked brown back. *Immature:* head stripes are brown and gray, not black and white.
Size: *L* 5½–7 in; *W* 9½ in.
Voice: several dialects have been identified; song is a highly variable, frequent *I-I-I-got-to-go-wee-wee-now!;* call is hard *pink* or high *seep.*
Status: common.
Habitat: woodlots, parkland edges, brushy tangles, riparian thickets; also open, weedy fields, lawns and roadsides.

Similar Birds

White-throated Sparrow
(p. 202)

Clay-colored Sparrow

bold black and white head stripes

gray face

2 white wing bars

gray, unstreaked underparts

Nesting: does not nest in Indiana; nests in northern and western North America; in a shrub, small conifer or on the ground; neat cup nest of vegetation is lined with fine materials; darkly marked, blue-green eggs are ⅞ x ⅝ in; female incubates 3–5 eggs for 11–14 days.

Did You Know?

The word *Zonotrichia* is Greek for "band" and "hair," a reference to the White-crowned Sparrow's head pattern.

Look For

During winter, good areas to look for White-crowns include the reclaimed strip mines in southwestern Indiana.

Dark-eyed Junco
Junco hyemalis

Juncos usually congregate in backyards with bird feeders and sheltering conifers—with such amenities at their disposal, more and more juncos are appearing in urban areas. These birds spend most of their time on the ground, snatching up seeds underneath bird feeders, and they are readily flushed from wooded trails and backyard feeders. • The junco is often called the "Snow Bird," and the species name, *hyemalis*, means "winter" in Greek.

Other ID: *Female:* gray-brown where male is slate gray.
Size: *L* 6–7 in; *W* 9 in.
Voice: song is a long, dry trill; call is a smacking *chip* note, often given in series.
Status: common from October to April.
Habitat: shrubby woodland borders and backyard feeders.

Similar Birds

Eastern Towhee
(p. 196)

Look For

This bird will flash its distinctive white outer tail feathers as it rushes for cover after being flushed.

pale pink bill

dark slate
gray overall

white outer
tail feathers

♂

white belly
and undertail
coverts

Nesting: does not nest in Indiana; nests in
northern and western North America; on the
ground, usually concealed; female builds a cup nest
of twigs, grass, bark shreds and moss; brown-
marked, whitish to bluish eggs are ¾ x ½ in;
female incubates 3–5 eggs for 12–13 days.

Did You Know?

There are five closely related Dark-eyed Junco subspecies in
North America that share similar habits but differ in coloration and range. It is the Slate-colored Junco subspecies that is
most common in our state, but occasionally the more colorful
western subspecies, the Oregon Junco, is also seen.

Northern Cardinal
Cardinalis cardinalis

A male Northern Cardinal displays his unforgettable, vibrant red head crest and raises his tail
when he is excited or agitated. He vigorously
defends his territory and will even attack his own
reflection in a window or hubcap! • The Northern
Cardinal is one of only a few bird species to
maintain strong pair bonds. Some couples sing to
each other year-round, while others join loose
flocks in fall, reestablishing pair bonds in spring.
These bonds are renewed with a courtship feeding:
the male offers a seed to the female, which she
then accepts and eats.

Other ID: *Male:* red overall. *Female:* brownish buff overall; fainter mask; red crest,
wings and tail.
Size: *L* 8–9 in; *W* 12 in.
Voice: call is a metallic *chip;* song is series of
clear, bubbly, whistled notes: *What cheer! What
cheer! birdie-birdie-birdie what cheer!*
Status: common.
Habitat: brushy thickets and shrubby tangles
along forest and woodland edges; backyards
and urban and suburban parks.

Similar Birds

Summer Tanager

Scarlet Tanager
(p. 194)

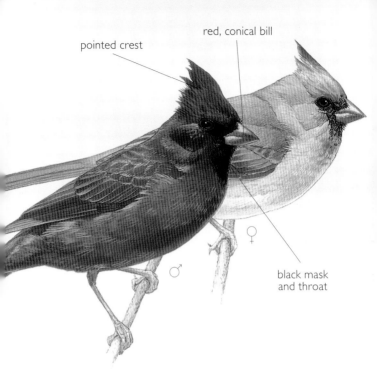

pointed crest

red, conical bill

♀

♂

black mask
and throat

Nesting: in a dense shrub, a vine tangle or
low in a coniferous tree; female builds an open
cup nest of twigs, grass and bark shreds;
brown-blotched, white to greenish white eggs
are 1 x ¾ in; female incubates 3–4 eggs for
12–13 days.

Did You Know?

The Northern Cardinal
is Indiana's state bird. Its
name refers to the red
robes of Roman Catholic
cardinals.

Look For

Northern Cardinals fly with
jerky movements and short
glides and have a preference
for sunflower seeds.

Indigo Bunting
Passerina cyanea

The vivid electric blue male Indigo Bunting is one of the most spectacular birds in Indiana. He is also a persistent singer, vocalizing even through the stifling heat of a summer day. A young male doesn't learn his couplet song from his parents, but rather from neighboring males during his first year on his own. • These birds arrive in April or May and favor raspberry thickets as nest sites. Dense, thorny stems keep most predators at a distance and the berries are a good food source. • Planting coneflowers, cosmos or foxtail grasses may attract Indigo Buntings to your backyard.

Other ID: black legs; no wing bars. *Breeding male:* bright blue overall; black lores. *Female:* soft brown overall; whitish throat. *Nonbreeding male:* mostly brown with blue blotches.
Size: L 5½ in; W 8 in.
Voice: song consists of paired warbled whistles: *fire-fire, where-where, here-here, see-it see-it;* call is a quick *spit.*
Status: common, especially in spring and summer.
Habitat: deciduous forest and woodland edges, regenerating forest clearings, orchards and shrubby fields.

Similar Birds

Blue Grosbeak

Eastern Bluebird
(p. 166)

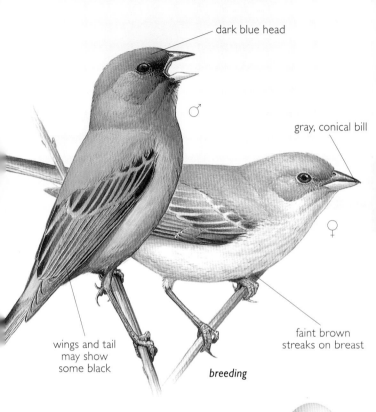

dark blue head

gray, conical bill

♂

♀

wings and tail
may show
some black

faint brown
streaks on breast

breeding

Nesting: in a small tree, shrub or within a vine tangle; female builds a cup nest of grass, leaves and bark strips; unmarked, white to bluish white eggs are ¾ x ½ in; female incubates 3–4 eggs for 12–13 days.

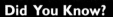

Did You Know?

Females choose the most melodious males as mates, because these males can usually establish territories with the finest habitat.

Look For

The Indigo Bunting will land midway on a stem of grass or a weed and shuffle slowly toward the seed head, bending down the stem to reach the seeds.

Red-winged Blackbird

Agelaius phoeniceus

The male Red-winged Blackbird wears his bright red shoulders like armor—together with his short, raspy song, they are key in defending his territory from rivals. In field experiments, males whose red shoulders were painted black soon lost their territories. • Nearly every cattail marsh worthy of note in Indiana hosts Red-winged Blackbirds during at least part of the year. • The female's cryptic coloration allows her to sit inconspicuously on her nest, blending in perfectly with the surroundings.

Other ID: *Male:* black overall. *Female:* mottled brown upperparts; pale eyebrow.
Size: L 7½–9 in; W 13 in.
Voice: song is a loud, raspy *konk-a-ree* or *ogle-reeeee;* calls include a harsh *check* and high *tseert;* female gives a loud *che-che-che chee chee chee.*
Status: common.
Habitat: cattail marshes, wet meadows and ditches, croplands and shoreline shrubs.

Similar Birds

Brewer's Blackbird

Rusty Blackbird

Brown-headed Cowbird
(p. 218)

red shoulder patch edged in yellow

faint, red shoulder patch

♀

heavily streaked underparts

♂

Nesting: colonial; in cattails or shoreline bushes; female builds an open cup nest of dried cattail leaves lined with fine grass; darkly marked, pale bluish green eggs are 1 x ¾ in; female incubates 3–4 eggs for 10–12 days.

Did You Know?

In fall, enormous flocks numbering in the hundreds of thousands form; a flock estimated to contain a million birds was seen in Lake County in 1961.

Look For

As he sings his *konk-a-ree* song, the male Red-winged Blackbird spreads his shoulders to display his bright red wing patch to rivals and potential mates.

Eastern Meadowlark
Sturnella magna

The drab dress of most female songbirds lends them protection during the breeding season, but the female Eastern Meadowlark uses a different strategy. Her V-shaped "necklace" and bright yellow throat and belly create a colorful distraction that leads predators away from the nest. A female flushed from the nest while incubating her eggs will often abandon the nest, and though she will never abandon her chicks, her extra vigilance following a threat usually results in less frequent feeding of nestlings.

Other ID: *Breeding:* yellow underparts; mottled brown upperparts; long, sharp bill; blackish crown stripes and eye line border pale eyebrow and median crown stripe; long, pinkish legs. *Nonbreeding:* paler plumage.
Size: *L* 9–9½ in; *W* 14 in.
Voice: song is a rich series of 2–8 melodic, clear, slurred whistles: *see-you at school-today* or *this is the year;* gives a rattling flight call and a high, buzzy *dzeart.*
Status: common in appropriate habitat.
Habitat: grassy meadows and pastures, some croplands, weedy fields and grassy roadsides.

Similar Birds

Western Meadowlark   Dickcissel

white jaw line

yellow lores

dark streaking on white sides and flanks

short, wide tail with white outer tail feathers

broad, black breast band

breeding

Nesting: in a concealed depression on the ground; female builds a domed grass nest, woven into surrounding vegetation; heavily spotted, white eggs are 1⅛ x ¾ in; female incubates 3–7 eggs for 13–15 days.

Did You Know?

Though the name suggests that this bird is a lark, its silhouette reveals it is actually a brightly colored member of the blackbird family.

Look For

The Eastern Meadowlark often whistles its proud song from fence posts and power lines. Its song is the best way to tell it apart from the Western Meadowlark.

Common Grackle
Quiscalus quiscula

The Common Grackle is a poor but spirited singer. Usually while perched in a shrub, a male grackle will slowly take a deep breath to inflate his breast, causing his feathers to spike outward, then close his eyes and give out a loud, strained *tssh-schleek*.
• In fall, large flocks of Common Grackles are found in rural areas. Smaller bands occasionally venture into urban neighbor-hoods, where they assert their domi-nance at backyard bird feeders.

Other ID: female is smaller, duller and browner than male. *Juvenile:* dull brown overall; dark eyes.
Size: *L* 11–13½ in; *W* 17 in.
Voice: song is a series of harsh, strained notes ending with a metallic squeak: *tssh-schleek* or *gri-de-leeek;* call is a quick, loud *swaaaack* or *chaack.*
Status: common.
Habitat: wetlands, hedgerows, fields, wet meadows, riparian woodlands and along the edges of coniferous forests and woodlands; also shrubby urban and suburban parks and gardens.

Similar Birds

Rusty Blackbird

Brewer's Blackbird

Red-winged Blackbird
(p. 212)

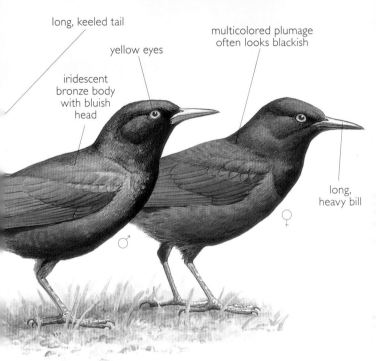

long, keeled tail

yellow eyes

iridescent
bronze body
with bluish
head

multicolored plumage
often looks blackish

long,
heavy bill

♂

♀

Nesting: singly or in small colonies; in a dense tree or shrub or in emergent vegetation; often near water; female builds a bulky, open cup nest of twigs, grass, plant fibers and mud and lines it with fine grass or feathers; brown-blotched, pale blue eggs are 1⅛ x ⅞ in; female incubates 4–5 eggs for 12–14 days.

Did You Know?

At night, grackles commonly roost with groups of European Starlings, Red-winged Blackbirds and even Brown-headed Cowbirds.

Look For

The Common Grackle has a long, heavy bill and a lengthy, wedge-shaped tail that trails behind in flight.

Brown-headed Cowbird
Molothrus ater

These nomads historically followed bison herds across the Great Plains (they now follow cattle), so they never stayed in one area long enough to build and tend a nest. Instead, cowbirds lay their eggs in other birds' nests, relying on the unsuspecting adoptive parents to incubate the eggs and feed the aggressive young. Orioles, warblers, vireos and tanagers are among the most affected species. Increased livestock farming and fragmentation of forests has encouraged the expansion of the cowbird's range. It is known to parasitize more than 140 bird species.

Other ID: dark eyes; thick, conical bill; short, squared tail.
Size: *L* 6–8 in; *W* 12 in.
Voice: song is a high, liquidy gurgle: *glug-ahl-whee* or *bubbloozeee;* call is a squeaky, high-pitched *seep, psee* or *wee-tse-tse* or fast, chipping *ch-ch-ch-ch-ch-ch.*
Status: common.
Habitat: agricultural and residential areas, usually fields, woodland edges, roadsides, fencelines, landfills and areas near cattle.

Similar Birds

Brewer's Blackbird

Red-winged Blackbird
(p. 212)

Rusty Blackbird

light brown with faint streaking

dark brown head

pale throat

nondescript plumage ♀

♂

iridescent, green-blue body plumage looks glossy black

Nesting: does not build a nest; female lays up to 30 eggs a year in the nests of other birds, usually 1 egg per nest; brown-speckled, whitish eggs are ⅞ x ⅝ in; eggs hatch after 10–13 days.

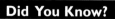

Did You Know?

When courting a female, the male cowbird points his bill upward to the sky, fans his tail and wings and utters a loud squeak.

Look For

When cowbirds feed in flocks, they hold their back ends up high, with their tails sticking straight up in the air.

Baltimore Oriole
Icterus galbula

With a flutelike song and a preference for the canopies of neighborhood trees, the Baltimore Oriole is difficult to spot, and a hanging pouch nest dangling in a bare tree in fall is sometimes the only evidence that the bird was there at all. The nests are deceptively strong and often remain intact through the harshest winters. • The male's plumage mirrors the colors of the coat of arms of Sir George Calvert, Baron of Baltimore, who established the first colony in Maryland.

Other ID: *Female:* olive brown upperparts (darkest on head); white wing bar.
Size: *L* 7–8 in; *W* 11½ in.
Voice: song consists of slow, clear whistles: *peter peter peter here peter;* calls include a 2-note *tea-too* and rapid chatter: *ch-ch-ch-ch-ch.*
Status: common.
Habitat: deciduous and mixed forests, particularly riparian woodlands, natural openings, shorelines, roadsides, orchards, gardens and parklands.

Similar Birds

Orchard Oriole

Scarlet Tanager
(p. 194)

black hood, back, wings and central tail feathers

white wing patch and feather edgings

♀

♂

dull yellow-orange under-parts and rump

bright orange underparts, shoulder, rump and outer tail feathers

Nesting: high in a deciduous tree; female builds a hanging pouch nest of grass, bark shreds and grapevines; darkly marked, pale gray to bluish white eggs are ⅞ x ⅝ in; female incubates 4–5 eggs for 12–14 days.

Did You Know?

Orioles spend more than half of each year in the tropics of Central and South America.

Look For

Spring migrants often arrive in a wave of color in early May. Many Hoosiers attract them to their backyards by posting halved oranges on the trees.

Purple Finch
Carpodacus purpureus

Despite this finch's name, its stunning plumage is more of a raspberry red than a shade of purple. Its musical *pik* call note is given frequently and is a good way to know if this finch is nearby. • A flat, raised, table-style feeding station and nearby tree cover are sure to attract the Purple Finch, and erecting a feeder may keep a small flock in your area over winter. • In breeding season, the male dances around the female, beating his wings rapidly until he gracefully lifts into the air.

Other ID: *Male:* pale bill; occasionally yellow to salmon pink coloration instead of red; reddish brown cheek; red rump; pale, unstreaked belly and undertail coverts. *Female:* white lower cheek stripe; unstreaked undertail coverts. *In flight:* notched tail.
Size: L 5–6 in; W 10 in.
Voice: song is a bubbly, continuous warble; call is a single, metallic *pik*.
Status: uncommon.
Habitat: *Breeding:* coniferous and mixed forests. *In migration* and *winter:* also deciduous forests, shrubby open areas and feeders.

Similar Birds

House Finch
(p. 224)

Red Crossbill

dark brown cheek and jaw line

pale eyebrow

heavily streaked underparts

stout, triangular bill

♀

♂

pale, unstreaked underparts

red wash over most of body

Nesting: does not nest in Indiana; nests in Canada and the western U.S.; on a conifer branch, far from the trunk; female builds a cup nest of twigs, grass and rootlets; darkly marked, pale greenish blue eggs are ¾ x ½ in; female incubates 4–5 eggs for 13 days.

Did You Know?

Purple Finches are especially fond of red maple, apple and elm flowers in spring.

Look For

Purple Finches stick to the outer branches of trees or glean the ground vegetation for seeds, buds, berries and insects.

House Finch

Carpodacus mexicanus

A native to western North America, the House Finch was brought to eastern parts of the continent as an illegally captured cage bird known as the "Hollywood Finch." In the early 1940s, New York pet shop owners released their birds to avoid prosecution and fines, and it is likely the descendants of those birds that have colonized our area. The first House Finches arrived in Indiana in the mid-1970s, and they are now commonly found throughout the continental U.S. and Hawaii.
• Only the resourceful House Finch has been aggressive and stubborn enough to successfully compete with the House Sparrow.

Other ID: streaked undertail coverts. *Female:* indistinct facial patterning; heavily streaked underparts.
Size: *L* 5–6 in; *W* 9½ in.
Voice: song is a bright, disjointed warble lasting about 3 seconds, often ending with a harsh *jeeer* or *wheer*; flight call is a sweet *cheer*, given singly or in series.
Status: common and widespread.
Habitat: cities, towns and agricultural areas.

Similar Birds

Purple Finch
(p. 222)

Red Crossbill

short bill

brown-
streaked back

bright red eyebrow,
forecrown, throat
and breast

♂

♀

heavy, brown
streaks on flanks

square tail

Nesting: in a cavity, a building, dense foliage
or an abandoned bird nest; open cup nest of
plant matter and other debris; pale blue,
spotted eggs are ¾ x ⁹/₁₆ in; female incubates
4–5 eggs for 12–14 days.

Did You Know?

The male House Finch's
plumage varies in color
from light yellow to bright
red, but females will
choose the reddest males
with which to breed.

Look For

In flight, the House Finch has
a square tail whereas the
similar-looking Purple Finch
has a sharply notched tail.

American Goldfinch

Carduelis tristis

Like vibrant rays of sunshine, American
Goldfinches cheerily flutter over weedy fields, gardens and along roadsides. It is hard to miss their
jubilant *po-ta-to-chip* call and their distinctive,
undulating flight style. • Because these acrobatic
birds regularly feed while hanging upside down,
finch feeders are designed with the seed openings
below the perches. These feeders discourage the
more aggressive House Sparrows, which feed
upright, from stealing the seeds. Use niger (thistle)
seeds or black-oil sunflower seeds to attract
American Goldfinches to your bird feeder.

Other ID: *Breeding male:* bright yellow body;
orange bill and legs. *Female:* yellow throat and
breast; yellow-green belly. *Nonbreeding male:* olive
brown back; yellow-tinged head; gray underparts.
Size: *L* 4½–5 in; *W* 9 in.
Voice: song is a long, varied series of trills,
twitters, warbles and hissing notes; calls
include *po-ta-to-chip* or *per-chic-or-ee* (often
delivered in flight) and a whistled *dear-me,
see-me.*
Status: common.
Habitat: weedy fields, woodland edges,
meadows, riparian areas, parks and gardens.

Similar Birds

Evening Grosbeak

Wilson's Warbler

yellow-green
upperparts

black cap
extends onto
forehead

black wings
with white
wing bars

♀

♂

breeding

white rump
and undertail
coverts

Nesting: in the fork of a deciduous tree;
compact cup nest of plant fibers, grass and
spider silk; pale bluish eggs are ⅝ x ½ in; female
incubates 4–6 eggs for 12–14 days.

Did You Know?

These birds nest in late
summer to ensure that
there is a dependable
source of seeds from this-
tles and dandelions to
feed their young.

Look For

American Goldfinches delight
in perching on late-summer
thistle heads or poking
through dandelion patches
in search of seeds.

House Sparrow
Passer domesticus

A black mask and "bib" adorn the male of this adaptive, aggressive species. The House Sparrow's tendency to usurp territory has led to a decline in native bird populations. This sparrow will even help itself to the convenience of another bird's home, such as a bluebird or Cliff Swallow nest or a Purple Martin house. • This abundant and conspicuous bird was introduced to North America in the 1850s as part of a plan to control the insects that were damaging grain and cereal crops; it first appeared in Indiana in 1867. As it turns out, these birds are largely vegetarian!

Other ID: *Breeding male:* gray crown; black bill; dark, mottled upperparts; gray underparts; white wing bar. *Female:* indistinct facial pattern; plain gray-brown overall; streaked upperparts.
Size: L 5½–6½ in; W 9½ in.
Voice: song is a plain, familiar *cheep-cheep-cheep-cheep;* call is a short *chill-up.*
Status: uncommon to abundant.
Habitat: townsites, urban and suburban areas, farmyards and agricultural areas, railroad yards and other developed areas.

Similar Birds

Harris's Sparrow

Look For

In spring, House Sparrows feast on the buds of fruit trees and will sometimes eat lettuce from a backyard garden.

buffy eyebrow

chestnut nape

black lore and "bib"

light gray cheek

♀

♂

breeding

grayish, unstreaked underparts

Nesting: often communal; in a birdhouse, ornamental shrub or natural cavity; pair builds a large dome nest of grass, twigs and plant fibers; gray-speckled, white to greenish eggs are ⅞ x ⅝ in; pair incubates 4–6 eggs for 10–13 days.

Did You Know?

The House Sparrow has successfully established itself in North America, owing in part to its high reproductive output. A pair may raise up to four clutches per year, with up to eight young per clutch.

Glossary

brood: *n.* a family of young from one hatching; *v.* to sit on eggs so as to hatch them.

cere: a fleshy area at the base of a bird's bill that contains the nostrils.

clutch: the number of eggs laid by the female at one time.

corvid: a member of the crow family (Corvidae); includes crows, jays, ravens and magpies.

crop: an enlargement of the esophagus; serves as a storage structure and (in pigeons) has glands that produce secretions.

dabbling: a foraging technique used by ducks, in which the head and neck are submerged but the body and tail remain on the water's surface; dabbling ducks can usually walk easily on land, can take off without running and have brightly colored speculums.

endangered: a species that is facing extirpation or extinction in all or part of its range.

extirpated: a species that no longer exists in the wild in a particular region but occurs elsewhere.

fledgling: a young bird that has left the nest but is dependent upon its parents.

flushing: a behavior in which frightened birds explode into flight in response to a disturbance.

leading edge: the front edge of the wing as viewed from below.

mantle: feathers of the back and upperside of folded wings.

molt: the periodic shedding and regrowth of worn feathers (often twice per year).

morph: one of several alternate plumages displayed by members of a species.

niche: an ecological role filled by a species.

passerine: a bird in the order Passeriformes, the bird order with the most species, representing nearly three-fifths of all living birds worldwide; includes all species from flycatchers to finches; also called perching birds or songbirds.

primaries: the outermost flight feathers.

raptor: a carnivorous (meat-eating) bird; includes eagles, hawks, falcons and owls.

riparian: refers to habitat along riverbanks.

rufous: rusty red in color.

sexual dimorphism: a difference in plumage, size or other characteristics between males and females of the same species.

special concern: a species that has characteristics that make it particularly sensitive to human disturbance, requires very specific or unique habitat or that requires careful monitoring because of its vulnerable status.

speculum: a brightly colored patch on the wings of many dabbling ducks.

threatened: a species likely to become endangered in the near future in all or part of its range.

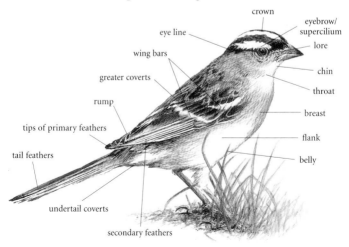

Checklist

The following checklist contains 291 species of birds that have been officially recorded as regular in Indiana. Species are grouped by family and listed in taxonomic order in accordance with the American Ornithologists' Union's *Check-list of North American Birds* (7th ed.) and its supplements. In addition, the following risk categories are also noted: extirpated (ex), endangered (en) and special concern (sc).

We wish to thank the Indian Bird Records Committee for their kind assistance in providing the information for this checklist.

Waterfowl
❏ Greater White-fronted
    Goose
❏ Snow Goose
❏ Ross's Goose
❏ Cackling Goose
❏ Canada Goose
❏ Mute Swan
❏ Trumpeter Swan (en)
❏ Tundra Swan
❏ Wood Duck
❏ Gadwall
❏ American Wigeon
❏ American Black Duck
❏ Mallard
❏ Blue-winged Teal
❏ Northern Shoveler
❏ Northern Pintail
❏ Green-winged Teal
❏ Canvasback
❏ Redhead
❏ Ring-necked Duck
❏ Greater Scaup
❏ Lesser Scaup
❏ Surf Scoter
❏ White-winged Scoter
❏ Black Scoter

❏ Long-tailed Duck
❏ Bufflehead
❏ Common Goldeneye
❏ Hooded Merganser
❏ Common Merganser
❏ Red-breasted Merganser
❏ Ruddy Duck

Grouse & Allies
❏ Gray Partridge (ex)
❏ Ring-necked Pheasant
❏ Ruffed Grouse
❏ Greater Prairie-Chicken (ex)
❏ Wild Turkey

Quails
❏ Northern Bobwhite

Loons
❏ Red-throated Loon
❏ Pacific Loon
❏ Common Loon

Grebes
❏ Pied-billed Grebe
❏ Horned Grebe
❏ Red-necked Grebe
❏ Eared Grebe
❏ Western Grebe

Pelicans
❑ American White Pelican

Cormorants
❑ Double-crested Cormorant

Herons
❑ American Bittern (en)
❑ Least Bittern (en)
❑ Great Blue Heron
❑ Great Egret (sc)
❑ Snowy Egret
❑ Little Blue Heron
❑ Cattle Egret
❑ Green Heron
❑ Black-crowned Night-Heron (en)
❑ Yellow-crowned Night-Heron (en)

Vultures
❑ Black Vulture
❑ Turkey Vulture

Hawks & Eagles
❑ Osprey (en)
❑ Bald Eagle (en)
❑ Northern Harrier (en)
❑ Sharp-shinned Hawk (sc)
❑ Cooper's Hawk
❑ Red-shouldered Hawk (sc)
❑ Broad-winged Hawk (sc)
❑ Red-tailed Hawk
❑ Rough-legged Hawk
❑ Golden Eagle

Falcons
❑ American Kestrel
❑ Merlin
❑ Peregrine Falcon (en)

Rails & Coots
❑ King Rail (en)
❑ Virginia Rail (en)
❑ Sora
❑ Common Moorhen (en)
❑ American Coot

Cranes
❑ Sandhill Crane (sc)
❑ Whooping Crane (en)

Plovers
❑ Black-bellied Plover
❑ American Golden-Plover
❑ Semipalmated Plover
❑ Piping Plover (en)
❑ Killdeer

Stilts & Avocets
❑ Black-necked Stilt
❑ American Avocet

Sandpipers & Allies
❑ Greater Yellowlegs
❑ Lesser Yellowlegs
❑ Solitary Sandpiper
❑ Willet
❑ Spotted Sandpiper
❑ Upland Sandpiper (en)
❑ Hudsonian Godwit
❑ Marbled Godwit
❑ Ruddy Turnstone
❑ Sanderling
❑ Semipalmated Sandpiper
❑ Least Sandpiper
❑ White-rumped Sandpiper
❑ Baird's Sandpiper
❑ Pectoral Sandpiper
❑ Purple Sandpiper

Northern Harrier

Sandhill Crane

Caspian
Tern

Eurasian
Collared-Dove

❏ Dunlin
❏ Stilt Sandpiper
❏ Buff-breasted Sandpiper
❏ Short-billed Dowitcher
❏ Long-billed Dowitcher
❏ Wilson's Snipe
❏ American Woodcock
❏ Wilson's Phalarope
❏ Red-necked Phalarope

Gulls & Terns
❏ Laughing Gull
❏ Franklin's Gull
❏ Bonaparte's Gull
❏ Ring-billed Gull
❏ Herring Gull
❏ Caspian Tern
❏ Common Tern
❏ Forster's Tern
❏ Least Tern (en)
❏ Black Tern (en)

Pigeons & Doves
❏ Rock Pigeon
❏ Eurasian Collared-Dove
❏ Mourning Dove

Parakeets
❏ Monk Parakeet

Cuckoos
❏ Black-billed Cuckoo
❏ Yellow-billed Cuckoo

Barn Owls
❏ Barn Owl (en)

Typical Owls
❏ Eastern Screech-Owl
❏ Great Horned Owl
❏ Snowy Owl
❏ Barred Owl

❏ Long-eared Owl
❏ Short-eared Owl (en)
❏ Northern Saw-whet Owl

Nightjars
❏ Common Nighthawk (sc)
❏ Chuck-will's-widow
❏ Whip-poor-will (sc)

Swifts
❏ Chimney Swift

Hummingbirds
❏ Ruby-throated
   Hummingbird

Kingfishers
❏ Belted Kingfisher

Woodpeckers
❏ Red-headed Woodpecker
❏ Red-bellied Woodpecker
❏ Yellow-bellied Sapsucker
❏ Downy Woodpecker
❏ Hairy Woodpecker
❏ Northern Flicker
❏ Pileated Woodpecker

Flycatchers
❏ Olive-sided Flycatcher
❏ Eastern Wood-Pewee
❏ Yellow-bellied Flycatcher
❏ Acadian Flycatcher
❏ Alder Flycatcher
❏ Willow Flycatcher
❏ Least Flycatcher
❏ Eastern Phoebe
❏ Great Crested Flycatcher
❏ Eastern Kingbird

Shrikes
❏ Loggerhead Shrike (en)
❏ Northern Shrike

Vireos
❑ White-eyed Vireo
❑ Bell's Vireo
❑ Yellow-throated Vireo
❑ Blue-headed Vireo
❑ Warbling Vireo
❑ Philadelphia Vireo
❑ Red-eyed Vireo

Jays & Crows
❑ Blue Jay
❑ American Crow

Larks
❑ Horned Lark

Martins & Swallows
❑ Purple Martin
❑ Tree Swallow
❑ Northern Rough-winged
   Swallow
❑ Bank Swallow
❑ Cliff Swallow
❑ Barn Swallow

Chickadees & Titmice
❑ Carolina Chickadee
❑ Black-capped Chickadee
❑ Tufted Titmouse

Nuthatches
❑ Red-breasted Nuthatch
❑ White-breasted Nuthatch

Creepers
❑ Brown Creeper

Wrens
❑ Carolina Wren
❑ House Wren
❑ Winter Wren
❑ Sedge Wren (en)
❑ Marsh Wren (en)

Kinglets
❑ Golden-crowned Kinglet
❑ Ruby-crowned Kinglet

Gnatcatchers
❑ Blue-gray Gnatcatcher

Thrushes
❑ Eastern Bluebird
❑ Veery
❑ Gray-cheeked Thrush
❑ Swainson's Thrush
❑ Hermit Thrush
❑ Wood Thrush
❑ American Robin
❑ Varied Thrush

Mimic Thrushes
❑ Gray Catbird
❑ Northern Mockingbird
❑ Brown Thrasher

Starlings
❑ European Starling

Pipits
❑ American Pipit

Waxwings
❑ Cedar Waxwing

Wood-warblers
❑ Blue-winged Warbler
❑ Golden-winged Warbler (en)
❑ Tennessee Warbler
❑ Orange-crowned Warbler
❑ Nashville Warbler
❑ Northern Parula
❑ Yellow Warbler
❑ Chestnut-sided Warbler
❑ Magnolia Warbler
❑ Cape May Warbler
❑ Black-throated Blue Warbler
❑ Yellow-rumped Warbler
❑ Black-throated Green
   Warbler
❑ Blackburnian Warbler
❑ Yellow-throated Warbler
❑ Pine Warbler
❑ Prairie Warbler
❑ Palm Warbler
❑ Bay-breasted Warbler
❑ Blackpoll Warbler
❑ Cerulean Warbler (sc)
❑ Black-and-white Warbler (sc)
❑ American Redstart
❑ Prothonotary Warbler
❑ Worm-eating Warbler (sc)
❑ Ovenbird
❑ Northern Waterthrush

- ❏ Louisiana Waterthrush
- ❏ Kentucky Warbler
- ❏ Connecticut Warbler
- ❏ Mourning Warbler
- ❏ Common Yellowthroat
- ❏ Hooded Warbler (sc)
- ❏ Wilson's Warbler
- ❏ Canada Warbler
- ❏ Yellow-breasted Chat

Tanagers
- ❏ Summer Tanager
- ❏ Scarlet Tanager

Sparrows & Allies
- ❏ Eastern Towhee
- ❏ American Tree Sparrow
- ❏ Chipping Sparrow
- ❏ Clay-colored Sparrow
- ❏ Field Sparrow
- ❏ Vesper Sparrow
- ❏ Lark Sparrow
- ❏ Savannah Sparrow
- ❏ Grasshopper Sparrow
- ❏ Henslow's Sparrow (en)
- ❏ Le Conte's Sparrow
- ❏ Nelson's Sharp-tailed Sparrow
- ❏ Fox Sparrow
- ❏ Song Sparrow
- ❏ Lincoln's Sparrow
- ❏ Swamp Sparrow
- ❏ White-throated Sparrow
- ❏ Harris's Sparrow
- ❏ White-crowned Sparrow
- ❏ Dark-eyed Junco

- ❏ Lapland Longspur
- ❏ Smith's Longspur
- ❏ Snow Bunting

Grosbeaks & Buntings
- ❏ Northern Cardinal
- ❏ Rose-breasted Grosbeak
- ❏ Blue Grosbeak
- ❏ Indigo Bunting
- ❏ Dickcissel

Blackbirds & Allies
- ❏ Bobolink
- ❏ Red-winged Blackbird
- ❏ Eastern Meadowlark
- ❏ Western Meadowlark (sc)
- ❏ Yellow-headed Blackbird (en)
- ❏ Rusty Blackbird
- ❏ Brewer's Blackbird
- ❏ Common Grackle
- ❏ Brown-headed Cowbird
- ❏ Orchard Oriole
- ❏ Baltimore Oriole

Finches
- ❏ Purple Finch
- ❏ House Finch
- ❏ Red Crossbill
- ❏ White-winged Crossbill
- ❏ Common Redpoll
- ❏ Pine Siskin
- ❏ American Goldfinch
- ❏ Evening Grosbeak

Old World Sparrows
- ❏ House Sparrow

American
Goldfinch

Common
Grackle

Select References

American Ornithologists' Union. 1998. *Check-list of North American Birds.* 7th ed. (and its supplements). American Ornithologists' Union, Washington, D.C.

Baicich, P.J. & C.J.O. Harrison. 2005. *Princeton Field Guides: Nests, Eggs and Nestlings of North American Birds.* 2nd ed. Princeton University Press, Princeton, NJ.

Choate, E.A. 1985. *The Dictionary of American Bird Names.* Rev. ed. Harvard Common Press, Cambridge, MA.

Cox, R.T. 1996. *Birder's Dictionary.* Falcon Publishing, Helena, MT.

Ehrlich, P.R., D.S. Dobkin & D. Wheye. 1988. *The Birder's Handbook: A Field Guide to the Natural History of North American Birds.* Simon & Schuster, New York, NY.

Jones, J.O. 1990. *Where The Birds Are: A Guide to All 50 States and Canada.* William Morrow and Company, New York, NY.

Kaufman, K. 1996. *Lives of North American Birds.* Houghton Mifflin Co., Boston, MA.

Kaufman, K. 2000. *Birds of North America.* Houghton Mifflin Co., New York, NY.

National Geographic Society. 2006. *Field Guide to the Birds of North America.* 5th ed. National Geographic Society, Washington, DC.

Mumford, R.E. & C.E. Keller. 1984. *The Birds of Indiana.* Indiana University Press, IN.

Peterson, R.T. 1996. *A Field Guide to the Birds: Including All Species Found in Eastern North America.* Houghton Mifflin Co., Boston, MA.

Sibley, D.A. 2000. *National Audubon Society: The Sibley Guide to Birds.* Alfred A. Knopf, New York, NY.

Sibley, D.A. 2001. *National Audubon Society: The Sibley Guide to Bird Life and Behavior.* Alfred A. Knopf, New York, NY.

Sibley, D.A. 2002. *Sibley's Birding Basics.* Alfred A. Knopf, New York, NY.

Index

A

Accipiter cooperii, 60
Agelaius phoeniceus, 212
Aix sponsa, 26
Anas
  discors, 30
  platyrhynchos, 28
Archilochus colubris, 114
Ardea
  alba, 48
  herodias, 46
Aythya affinis, 32

B

Baeolophus bicolor, 152
Blackbird, Red-winged, 212
Bluebird, Eastern, 166
Bobwhite, Northern, 40
Bombycilla cedrorum, 180
Branta canadensis, 22
Bubo virginianus, 106
Bucephala clangula, 34
Bunting, Indigo, 210
Buteo jamaicensis, 62
Butorides virescens, 50

C

Calidris
  alba, 78
  melanotos, 80
Caprimulgus vociferus, 112
Cardinal, Northern, 208
Cardinalis cardinalis, 208
Carduelis tristis, 226
Carpodacus
  mexicanus, 224
  purpureus, 222
Catbird, Gray, 172
Cathartes aura, 52
Certhia americana, 156
Ceryle alcyon, 116
Charadrius vociferus, 74
Chen caerulescens, 20
Chickadee, Carolina, 150
Chordeiles minor, 110
Circus cyaneus, 58

Coccyzus americanus, 102
Colaptes auratus, 124
Colinus virginianus, 40
Collared-Dove, Eurasian, 98
Columba livia, 96
Contopus virens, 128
Coot, American, 70
Cormorant, Double-crested, 44
Corvus brachyrhynchos, 140
Cowbird, Brown-headed, 218
Crane, Sandhill, 72
Creeper, Brown, 156
Crow, American, 140
Cuckoo, Yellow-billed, 102
Cyanocitta cristata, 138
Cygnus olor, 24

D

Dendroica
  coronata, 184
  fusca, 186
  petechia, 182
Dove, Mourning, 100
Dryocopus pileatus, 126
Duck, Wood, 26
Dumetella carolinensis, 172

E, F

Eagle, Bald, 56
Egret, Great, 48
Eremophila alpestris, 142
Falco
  peregrinus, 66
  sparverius, 64
Falcon, Peregrine, 66
Finch
  House, 224
  Purple, 222
Flicker, Northern, 124
Flycatcher, Great Crested, 132
Fulica americana, 70

G

Geothlypis trichas, 192
Gnatcatcher, Blue-gray, 164
Goldeneye, Common, 34
Goldfinch, American, 226

Goose
  Canada, 22
  Snow, 20
Grackle, Common, 216
Grebe, Pied-billed, 42
Grus canadensis, 72
Gull
  Bonaparte's, 84
  Herring, 88
  Ring-billed, 86

H

Haliaeetus leucocephalus, 56
Harrier, Northern, 58
Hawk
  Cooper's, 60
  Red-tailed, 62
Heron
  Great Blue, 46
  Green, 50
Hirundo rustica, 148
Hummingbird, Ruby-throated, 114
Hydroprogne caspia, 90
Hylocichla mustelina, 168

I, J

Icterus galbula, 220
Jay, Blue, 138
Junco hyemalis, 206
Junco, Dark-eyed, 206

K

Kestrel, American, 64
Killdeer, 74
Kingbird, Eastern, 134
Kingfisher, Belted, 116
Kinglet, Ruby-crowned, 162

L

Lark, Horned, 142
Larus
  argentatus, 88
  delawarensis, 86
  philadelphia, 84
Lophodytes cucullatus, 36

M

Mallard, 28
Martin, Purple, 144
Meadowlark, Eastern, 214

Megascops asio, 104
Melanerpes
  carolinus, 120
  erythrocephalus, 118
Meleagris gallopavo, 38
Melospiza melodia, 200
Merganser, Hooded, 36
Mimus polyglottos, 174
Mockingbird, Northern, 174
Molothrus ater, 218
Myiarchus crinitus, 132

N, O

Nighthawk, Common, 110
Nuthatch, White-breasted, 154
Oriole, Baltimore, 220
Osprey, 54
Ovenbird, 190
Owl
  Barred, 108
  Great Horned, 106

P

Pandion haliaetus, 54
Passer domesticus, 228
Passerina cyanea, 210
Phalacrocorax auritus, 44
Phoebe, Eastern, 130
Picoides pubescens, 122
Pigeon, Rock, 96
Pipilo erythrophthalmus, 196
Piranga olivacea, 194
Podilymbus podiceps, 42
Poecile carolinensis, 150
Polioptila caerulea, 164
Porzana carolina, 68
Progne subis, 144

Q, R

Quiscalus quiscula, 216
Redstart, American, 188
Regulus calendula, 162
Robin, American, 170

S

Sanderling, 78
Sandpiper, Pectoral, 80
Sayornis phoebe, 130
Scaup, Lesser, 32
Scolopax minor, 82

Screech-Owl, Eastern, 104
Seiurus aurocapilla, 190
Setophaga ruticilla, 188
Sialia sialis, 166
Sitta carolinensis, 154
Sora, 68
Sparrow
  American Tree, 198
  House, 228
  Song, 200
  White-crowned, 204
  White-throated, 202
Spizella arborea, 198
Starling, European, 178
Sterna
  forsteri, 94
  hirundo, 92
Streptopelia decaocto, 98
Strix varia, 108
Sturnella magna, 214
Sturnus vulgaris, 178
Swallow
  Barn, 148
  Tree, 146
Swan, Mute, 24

T

Tachycineta bicolor, 146
Tanager, Scarlet, 194
Teal, Blue-winged, 30
Tern
  Caspian, 90
  Common, 92
  Forster's, 94
Thrasher, Brown, 176
Thrush, Wood, 168
Thryothorus ludovicianus, 158
Titmouse, Tufted, 152
Towhee, Eastern, 196
Toxostoma rufum, 176
Tringa flavipes, 76
Troglodytes aedon, 160
Turdus migratorius, 170
Turkey, Wild, 38
Tyrannus tyrannus, 134

U, V, W

Vireo olivaceus, 136
Vireo, Red-eyed, 136

Vulture, Turkey, 52
Warbler
  Blackburnian, 186
  Yellow, 182
  Yellow-rumped, 184
Waxwing, Cedar, 180
Whip-poor-will, 112
Woodcock, American, 82
Woodpecker
  Downy, 122
  Pileated, 126
  Red-bellied, 120
  Red-headed, 118
Wood-Pewee, Eastern, 128
Wren
  Carolina, 158
  House, 160

X, Y, Z

Yellowlegs, Lesser, 76
Yellowthroat, Common, 192
Zenaida macroura, 100
Zonotrichia
  albicollis, 202
  leucophrys, 204

Goose
  Canada, 22
  Snow, 20
Grackle, Common, 216
Grebe, Pied-billed, 42
Grus canadensis, 72
Gull
  Bonaparte's, 84
  Herring, 88
  Ring-billed, 86

H

Haliaeetus leucocephalus, 56
Harrier, Northern, 58
Hawk
  Cooper's, 60
  Red-tailed, 62
Heron
  Great Blue, 46
  Green, 50
Hirundo rustica, 148
Hummingbird, Ruby-throated, 114
Hydroprogne caspia, 90
Hylocichla mustelina, 168

I, J

Icterus galbula, 220
Jay, Blue, 138
Junco hyemalis, 206
Junco, Dark-eyed, 206

K

Kestrel, American, 64
Killdeer, 74
Kingbird, Eastern, 134
Kingfisher, Belted, 116
Kinglet, Ruby-crowned, 162

L

Lark, Horned, 142
Larus
  argentatus, 88
  delawarensis, 86
  philadelphia, 84
Lophodytes cucullatus, 36

M

Mallard, 28
Martin, Purple, 144
Meadowlark, Eastern, 214

Megascops asio, 104
Melanerpes
  carolinus, 120
  erythrocephalus, 118
Meleagris gallopavo, 38
Melospiza melodia, 200
Merganser, Hooded, 36
Mimus polyglottos, 174
Mockingbird, Northern, 174
Molothrus ater, 218
Myiarchus crinitus, 132

N, O

Nighthawk, Common, 110
Nuthatch, White-breasted, 154
Oriole, Baltimore, 220
Osprey, 54
Ovenbird, 190
Owl
  Barred, 108
  Great Horned, 106

P

Pandion haliaetus, 54
Passer domesticus, 228
Passerina cyanea, 210
Phalacrocorax auritus, 44
Phoebe, Eastern, 130
Picoides pubescens, 122
Pigeon, Rock, 96
Pipilo erythrophthalmus, 196
Piranga olivacea, 194
Podilymbus podiceps, 42
Poecile carolinensis, 150
Polioptila caerulea, 164
Porzana carolina, 68
Progne subis, 144

Q, R

Quiscalus quiscula, 216
Redstart, American, 188
Regulus calendula, 162
Robin, American, 170

S

Sanderling, 78
Sandpiper, Pectoral, 80
Sayornis phoebe, 130
Scaup, Lesser, 32
Scolopax minor, 82

Screech-Owl, Eastern, 104
Seiurus aurocapilla, 190
Setophaga ruticilla, 188
Sialia sialis, 166
Sitta carolinensis, 154
Sora, 68
Sparrow
  American Tree, 198
  House, 228
  Song, 200
  White-crowned, 204
  White-throated, 202
Spizella arborea, 198
Starling, European, 178
Sterna
  forsteri, 94
  hirundo, 92
Streptopelia decaocto, 98
Strix varia, 108
Sturnella magna, 214
Sturnus vulgaris, 178
Swallow
  Barn, 148
  Tree, 146
Swan, Mute, 24

T

Tachycineta bicolor, 146
Tanager, Scarlet, 194
Teal, Blue-winged, 30
Tern
  Caspian, 90
  Common, 92
  Forster's, 94
Thrasher, Brown, 176
Thrush, Wood, 168
Thryothorus ludovicianus, 158
Titmouse, Tufted, 152
Towhee, Eastern, 196
Toxostoma rufum, 176
Tringa flavipes, 76
Troglodytes aedon, 160
Turdus migratorius, 170
Turkey, Wild, 38
Tyrannus tyrannus, 134

U, V, W

Vireo olivaceus, 136
Vireo, Red-eyed, 136

Vulture, Turkey, 52
Warbler
  Blackburnian, 186
  Yellow, 182
  Yellow-rumped, 184
Waxwing, Cedar, 180
Whip-poor-will, 112
Woodcock, American, 82
Woodpecker
  Downy, 122
  Pileated, 126
  Red-bellied, 120
  Red-headed, 118
Wood-Pewee, Eastern, 128
Wren
  Carolina, 158
  House, 160

X, Y, Z

Yellowlegs, Lesser, 76
Yellowthroat, Common, 192
Zenaida macroura, 100
Zonotrichia
  albicollis, 202
  leucophrys, 204